FACTS AND INTERPRETATION

A Prayer Manual for Prayer Warriors

FACTS AND INTERPRETATION

A Prayer Manual for Prayer Warriors

Charles Misori

ARPress
45 Dan Road Suite 5
Canton MA 02021

Hotline:	1(888) 821-0229
Fax:	1(508) 545-7580

Ordering Information:

Quantity sales. Special discounts are available on quantity purchases by corporations, associations, and others. For details, contact the publisher at the address above.

Printed in the United States of America.

ISBN-13:	Paperback	979-8-89356-212-5
	eBook	979-8-89356-213-2

Library of Congress Control Number: 2024907672

To Jesus Christ of Nazareth, Who continues to teach me through His Spirit and Word that the most important prayer in this life and the greatest prayer you can pray is the prayer that He Himself prayed to His Father, which He says, "Nevertheless, not my will, but thine be done" (Luke 22:42).

Also to my parents: Enoch Bokwe Misori and Catherine Ngonde Nekongo Misori. Both of them are deceased.

CONTENTS

FOREWORD

The book you hold in your hands stems from a deep concern for the salvation of those who live "without Christ, being aliens from the commonwealth of Israel and strangers from the covenants of promise, having no hope and without God in the world" (Ephesians 2:12).

Charles Misori invites his readers not to limit their petitions to earthly interests. He encourages them to engage in intercessory prayer on behalf of souls in need of eternal salvation. He addresses passionate advocacy in favor of a life that reflects our profession and petition. He challenges the church's prayer warriors to minister as devoted priests who "weep between the porch and the altar," imploring the Lord to spare His people from reproach while they engage in the mission of seeking the lost (Joel 2:17).

The present opuscule emphasizes the importance of prayer as a powerful weapon in the battle for soul winning. It is a sine qua non for any Christian who is serious about the Great Commission: Go therefore and make disciples of all the nations, baptizing them in the name of the Father and of the Son and the Holy Spirit (Matthew 28:19).

Prayer warriors will significantly benefit from the reading of this work that indicates the pitfalls of intercessory prayers and the way to circumvent them.

Agniel Samson, ThD
Retired Dean and Professor of New Testament Studies,
Biblical Languages, and World Religions
School of Theology, Oakwood University

ACKNOWLEDGMENTS

The theme of this book is the Holy Spirit and His influence on our prayer life as believers. We cannot live a fulfilled life as intercessors or prayer warriors without His power in our lives. So it is natural that I acknowledge Him as the one Who made this book possible.

I would also like to recognize Ms. Courtney Braggs at the Public Library in Huntsville, Alabama, for typing the manuscript until it was ready for publication.

In particular, this book was under the perceptive and insightful eye of a humble theologian, Dr. Agniel Samson, a retired dean at the Oakwood University College of Theology. My debt to him is unpayable.

In addition, I would like to thank the editors at ARPress, for their masterful editorial discernment, unaffected seriousness, and their considerable enthusiasm for this project. My gratitude to them is unmeasurable.

I am also pleased to acknowledge my daughters, Ruth, Naomi, and Miriam, for their influence on my life. They are good girls.

It is, of course, quintessential for the author to acknowledge his wife's contribution to a book. But in my case, this contribution extends far beyond typical limits. Ruth Ete Sakwe Misori helped me at every phase of the book, and this is an opportunity for me to say how grateful I am for our relationship.

INTRODUCTION

It is difficult to exaggerate the importance of prayer in the life of a Christian. However, we have in our churches today, more than a few members who still harbor a misunderstanding about the power of prayer. I have no hesitation in saying that any failure in life in general, but especially in the life of a Christian, can be traced to a failure of prayer. Someone has said that when we remedy the prayer life of the people of God, we fix what is wrong with Christians and churches and open the way for every needed blessing.

This writer does not pose as an authority on prayer, but I believe that Christians everywhere express a need for more power to practice their Christian values. Many Christians believe that the ability to serve Christ, witness for Christ, and engage in spiritual warfare is still available to them but do not know how to access that power.

According to Andrew Murray (a prayer warrior of yesteryears), God's children can conquer Satan and anything and everything through prayer.

This writing is not a treatise on prayer. However, I attempt to unlock another perspective, another layer of evidence, or interpretation about prayer that is missing through either neglect or lack of knowledge. It is no longer a truism that the one entity that knows the impact of prayer on his activities more than anyone else is Satan. That is why he works every minute of every day to discourage praying people from praying because he cannot pray. *Satan fears prayer more than anything else that you or I can do. Prayer poses the greatest danger to the purposes and plans of Satan.* Importantly, prayer is the most excellent avenue or instrumentality for spiritual power and spiritual victory as a Christian.

On several occasions and in many ways, Jesus Christ demonstrated "that without faith, it is impossible to please God" (Hebrews 11:6). *And true faith expresses itself in prayer. The adequate expression of faith is a prayer that focuses on praise.*

If you were baptized in the name of God the Father, God the Son, and God the Holy Ghost like most of us, then you are a trinitarian, which means that you believe in the coequal nature of the Godhead. They all existed before we came into the scene, and they have equal power and authority. However, because our ideas about this triune God are too human, we tend to foster a certain misunderstanding about their various roles and functions. In this book, I endeavor to show that my prayer life and your prayer life, but especially the life of a prayer warrior, is made better every day by your constant and daily contact with God the Holy Spirit. That is my premise. We need an intelligent appreciation of the power of the Holy Spirit in all aspects of our lives as Christians. Jesus is the King of kings and Lord of lords. He is the Savior and mediator of the world. He paid the price for us to gain eternal life. We make our petitions in His name. He is preeminent in all things. He foresees our trials, and as our advocate prays for us. Simon, Simon, Satan has desired to have you, but I have prayed for you with a touching frankness. However, before He left the world scene as we know it, He bequeathed the Holy Spirit to us and said, "I am sending the comforter who will tell you all things" (John 14:26) as it were to continue His ministry. The Holy Spirit is indispensable in everything Christians do, serving or bringing glory to Christ and developing an effective prayer life. The mandate of the Holy Spirit, as I understand it, is to continue the ministry of Jesus Christ. A daily and frequent conversation with the Holy Spirit who dwells in you produces the character of Jesus Christ in you (1 Corinthians 3:16) and allows you to see things from His perspective. His goal is to reproduce Christ in you. Apostle Paul says in Romans 8:11 that the Spirit that raised Jesus from the dead dwells in you. Furthermore, you are considered a son and daughter of God only as you are led (*daily*) by the Spirit of God (Romans 8:14).

The venerated Charles Spurgeon claims that there is no spiritual good in all the world of which *he* is not the author and sustainer. John says, "Behold what manner of love the Father has bestowed upon us that we should be called the children of God. Therefore, 'the world knoweth us not because it knew Him not'" (John 3:1). Did you know that only God can speak for Himself, and only the Holy Spirit can communicate this knowledge to us? That is how critical He is to our walk with God. The attention point is that most of us are unaware that we are in the Holy Spirit dispensation. Jesus commended Peter following his answer to the question: Who do men say that I am? That response from the Master should strike the reflecting reader that the Holy Spirit is imperative in everything we do. Jesus said to Peter and us that his answer did not come from him but the Spirit of God. To receive Jesus Christ as your Savior is to receive the Holy Spirit implicitly. And you cannot receive Jesus unless God the Father draws you. I have found comfort in depending on the Holy Spirit in my praying, and I am willing to share this insight as a guide. I am also not trying to improve on the ministry of the Holy Spirit. Nobody can. With the help of the Holy Spirit, I hope to reveal where the church has departed from the source of its power in reaching the world for Christ. *The church will not make inroads into the world unless it believes in the power of the Holy Spirit profoundly.* And believe it or not, it begins with an improved understanding of the role of the Holy Spirit in the prayer life of the individual Christian and the church itself. There is a growing disposition among experts on prayer to write books about how to pray, steps to a better prayer life, and so on. That is not my objective. Instead, I hope that these hints will awaken you, the reader, to apply these interpretations to your own life and experience what it all means. Prayer should be the most significant fact of our lives because it involves us. Our prayers are formed and shaped by the needs and challenges that confront us on a daily basis as individuals and as a community. Believe it or not, prayer without the Holy Spirit is ineffective. All biblical references are from the King James translation unless indicated.

Elder Charles Misori, PhD
Huntsville, Alabama
December 27, 2016

CHAPTER 1
Prayer and the Knowledge of God

God is not a respecter of persons, but I must say He is a respecter of conditions. One of the conditions for an effective prayer life for a prayer warrior is knowledge of God (Hosea 4:6; Proverbs 5:23; Job 36:12). My view is that it is the calling of every believer to know God for themselves. I do not mean that a mortal being can know everything that there is to know about the Almighty God. Instead, what I mean is a certain familiarity that borders on intimacy. It is one thing to know your Bible, but it is quite another to know the God of the Bible. *Insufficient understanding of God's character is one of the most significant weaknesses in our prayer life. People who know God trust Him (Daniel 3:1–18; Psalm 89:15–16, Psalm 9:10).* Faith in His character increases your knowledge of God, and this increased knowledge leads to implicit trust in Him. Trust makes obedience effortless. That is the sequence. This knowledge allows you to know that nobody or circumstance can thwart His plans for you (Job: 42:1–2; 2 Chronicles 20:6, Proverbs 19:21, 16:4, 21:30; 1 Samuel 2:10; Exodus 15:6–7; Psalm 68:1–2; Isaiah 8:10, 14:27; Job 34:29). Even man's failures do not frustrate His plans (see Romans 11:1–12).

Some wicked Jews (forty of them) took an oath that they would neither eat nor drink until they had killed Paul. Now, this was their plan. God had a different plan for Paul, and His plan prevailed. He rescued Paul through a series of events that encapsulates this notion that nobody can thwart God's plans (Acts 23:10–35). So when you pray, remember to remind yourself that nothing can frustrate His plans. Obstacles can stand in your way, but nothing can thwart His plans**.** *Know that the devil is more unable than unwilling to abort the Creator's plans and know that as you know your name. This our God, and I mean the God of Abraham, Isaac, and Jacob, has no problems, only plans. Think about that. What we may sometimes and often consider problems are plans from God.*

There are certain truths about God that no one can change. One of them is that nothing can thwart His plans for His people, including every contingency. He always remembers His covenant with His people. God's plan is for all creation, things in heaven and earth, visible and invisible, thrones, dominions, rulers, and authorities (Colossians 1:16). I encourage you to read Genesis 37 and look at everything that happened in Joseph's story. It was not a coincidence that they informed him of his brothers' whereabout (Genesis 37:14–17); the passing caravan was not a coincidence either (Genesis 37:25–28). Joseph was the flower of the flock.

I must stress this characteristic of God because your knowledge of God's immutable character emboldens your prayer life. And you cannot know God without the power of the Holy Spirit. We need to understand what God has said about Himself, what He has said about us believers, and what He has said about the devil. Those teachings will be fundamental as we pray to God, who likes us to think about His character. This view holds that prayer is talking to God about God.

George Muller in England served the needs of young orphans who had lost their parents during the war through prayer and nothing more. On one occasion, the children did not have food that morning. His prayer on behalf of the children was, "Lord, you said in your Word that you are 'a father to the fatherless.' Now fulfill your covenant that you are indeed a father to the fatherless since these children are fatherless and do not have food to eat this morning" (Psalm 68:5). God's response was swift and immediate. A truck distributing bread and milk got stuck in the snow just in front of the orphanage. The truck driver had no choice but to offer the bread and milk to the children because the bread and milk would have spoiled. Why was God's response so immediate? Because the honor and reputation of His name and Word were at stake. Do you know what He says about you and me? Listen to Him in 2 Timothy 4:18, "The Lord will deliver me from every evil work and preserve me into His heavenly kingdom. To Him be glory forever." When you are being harassed or bedeviled by the evil one, remind Him about what the Lord said in His promise about you. We will talk more about that.

However, it is not enough just to know His character. Applying this knowledge of His character to the challenges in your life is what makes your prayer life powerful. *Your knowledge of God impacts your daily look and outlook on life. And it is the power of the Holy Spirit that makes us understand* His abilities and His everlasting love. For He says, "I have loved you with an everlasting love" (Jeremiah 31:3). You know for a fact that He is the one who wakes you up every morning, not the alarm clock. "For thou hast lifted me up" (Psalm 30:1). He preserves your movement. "The Lord shall preserve thy going out and thy coming in from this time forth and even forevermore" (Psalm 121:8).

There is one fundamental truth that none of us can ignore. It is an unassailable fact, and that is, you cannot be satisfied in this life without knowing God. For a man has learned nothing unless he has grasped the fact that he needs God. The African theologian of yesteryears, Augustine, claimed that God created a vacuum in us, and until He occupies that inner sanctum, we will be without rest. And the more you taste His goodness, the more you thirst for more. It is a spiritual principle that the closer you get to Him, the more you desire to be in His presence. There is a certain reciprocity that I have experienced, and I am sure most born-again or prayer warriors have experienced as well. The more you pray and feel His presence and move to a spiritual realm, the more you want to pray. Prayer leads you to God, and while you are there, all you want to do is pray. God knows you because He created you, and He wants you to know Him as well. And this knowledge becomes very pertinent as you pray to Him daily. Importantly, this knowledge is experienced and amassed as you daily interact with His Word. A healthy intersection between you, the Holy Spirit, and His Word redounds to a relationship, which is the fulcrum of prayer. Prayer is rooted and grounded in the soil of relationship. *Prayer is a relationship.*

The more you nurture this relationship through consistency, the more you begin to discover that your God is a covenant-keeping God (Deuteronomy 7:9; Jer 32:38). This knowledge increases and releases your unreserved confidence in Him and His Word. First, He gives you His Word (Jeremiah 1:9), then He says, "speak my words, and I will perform what I have pledged to do in my word" (Jeremiah 1:12). The upshot of this confidence is that prayer becomes a delight in your daily walk. When you pray, reminding Him of His promises, your question becomes: Lord, would you be faithful to your covenant? Again, His

Word says that no promise He made ever failed to be fulfilled (1 Kings 8:56; Joshua 21:45). *The Word of God is the gateway to knowing the God of heaven, and it is the Holy Spirit that opens your understanding of the Word. You can behold the wondrous things of the Law only as He opens your mind.* It reveals the heart of God. And His Word becomes your guide in life (Psalm 119:130). Once you discover the power of God's Word (Hebrews 4:12), then your response and prayer becomes, "Lord, grant to me the blessing of a life whose greatest desire is to know you more and more, please, you more and more, and my greatest hunger and my highest ambition are to glorify you as my God." *Do not let anything diminish your consistent contact with the Word of God for that is where the power is* (Ecclesiastes 8:4). *When you know God, you will be more concerned with His glory than anything else when you pray.*

There is a story about the Apostle Paul before his conversion that he knew God as the living God who is mighty to overrule *all* things. However, there came a time when what he knew about God could not save him from his disgust and despair, even though he was a man of extraordinary intellectual power. Applying what you know about God makes a huge difference in your daily walk with Him and your prayer life.

To be forewarned is to be forearmed. Do not be fooled by anyone who claims to have served in ministry for several years and therefore can speak authoritatively for God. He says my ways are not your ways, and my thoughts are not your thoughts (Isaiah 55:8–9). *My appeal is to know Him for yourself.* That is the definition that Jesus gave for eternal life (John 17:3). Someone has said that if you know Jesus Christ of Nazareth personally the way that you are supposed to know Him, then what you do not know is irrelevant, but if you do not know Jesus Christ personally the way you ought to know Him, then whatever you know is nugatory. "Acquaint *now* thyself with *Him*, and be at peace, thereby good shall come unto thee" (Job 22:21). Or instead, ask Him to reveal Himself to you as you pray to Him daily. And it is the Holy Spirit that does that.

An older retired minister of the gospel made this point in one of his sermons. He told the story of one of his elders who experienced severe chest pains. They rushed him to the hospital. The pastor visited the elder in the hospital and prayed for him. A few days later, the doctors were not confident of his prognosis, so the pastor went back, and this time, he prayed and anointed him with olive oil. Later that day, he received a call that the elder was suddenly doing very well after he prayed for him at the hospital. As it turned out, this elder was discharged from the hospital the next day. About a month later, another elder fell ill, and this same pastor went to the hospital, prayed for this elder, and did the same thing, anointing him with oil as the Bible prescribes. However, no sooner did he leave the room after praying than the elder took his last breath. *Anyone who knows everything about God must be God.* Since his prayer relieved the other elder, the retired pastor thought that he would say the same prayer, which would bring healing to the sick man. The pride that you know God more than others is hazardous.

In a prayer meeting, they asked another gospel minister why lots of people were dying from cancer. His response was, "Because people are not obeying God." He quoted Exodus 15:26, "If you diligently heed the voice of the *Lord* your God and do what is right in His sight, give ear to His commandments and keep all His statutes, I will put none of the diseases on you which I have brought on the Egyptians." In other words, sickness and death resulted from disobedience. That was the popular and prevailing view among the Jews in the first century when Jesus Christ was on the scene. Jesus disabused this view in John 9:1–12 when his disciples asked who sinned that the man was born blind, him, or his parents. Jesus responded that none of them sinned. However, the man was born blind so that the works of God may be made manifest in him (verse 3). You will meet people, especially some clergy, who want to leave the impression that they know God and explain Him based on their many years in the ministry.

Listen to them but always confer with the Holy Spirit. Their own experiences determine the limits of their boundaries. Only the Holy Spirit can see the end from the beginning. He will teach you all things; that was the teaching from the Master Jesus Christ of Nazareth. If you pretend to have all the answers, then you are making yourself God, and we have just one God, and that is the one who came and died for you and me on Calvary, *Jesus Christ.* I am God, and there is none other, and apart from me, there is no other God (Isaiah 45:5; 44:6–8; Psalm 135:5–6). Then shall we know, if we follow on to know the *Lord* (Hosea 6:3). If any man does His will, he shall know Him (John

7:17). And "the people that do know their God shall be strong and do exploits" (Daniel 11:32). *In the end, it is not the amount of knowledge you have but the usage you make of that knowledge. Ask yourself: What place have I given this knowledge of God in my heart, and what connection does this knowledge have with the motives, principles, and ruling ideas of my daily life? In other words, does my understanding of God form, inform, and brace my walk with God?* That is the question that prayer warriors must ask and answer. "Seek ye the Lord while He may be found, call ye upon Him while He is near" (Isaiah 55:6). *You cannot seek the Lord unless the Holy Spirit initiates that process.*

Today, seek Him with a desire to know Him better. Know His character: faithful, merciful, holy, just, all-powerful, wise, great, graceful, and His love and loving-kindness. These do not change, and as a prayer warrior, that is what you cling to when you pray (Malachi 3:6). Communion with God is profoundly personal, and that is the surest means of knowing God. In Colossians 3:10, Paul tells us to "put on the new (nature) who is renewed in (the) knowledge of" our Creator and *become like Him. And that is the goal, to know Him and to become like Him. Prayer warriors who know God are not afraid of anything from the enemy's camp.* The three Hebrew boys remind us of God's faithfulness to those who know Him. *Remember that your knowledge of God is the secret of your spiritual life*, and it presents and represents your only safeguard against error and sin. Jesus tells us that "a man can receive nothing unless it is given to Him from Heaven" (John 3:27; 1 Corinthians 4:7). Ask the Holy Spirit to release the wisdom and power to know God for the glory of His name. When you do, please do not trifle with the truth. Do not let your self-interest color your prayer to know God. Instead, let it be for the glory of God. Holy Spirit, please do it for me, and I thank you.

Hymn:

God will take care of you
Be not dismayed whate'er betide,
God will take care of you.
Beneath His wings of love abide,
God will take care of you.
Refrain
God will take of you, through every day,
O'er all the way
He will take care of you; God will take care of you.

CHAPTER 2
Prayer and the Will of God

Scripture says, "In all things, give thanks for this is the will of God in Christ Jesus concerning you" (1 Thessalonians 5:18). In response to a question by His disciples, Jesus taught them the Lord's prayer found in Matthew 6. In verse 10, Jesus says, "Thy kingdom come; thy will be done on earth as it is in heaven." Jesus is praying to His Father and is asking us to pray in like manner. However, a careful study and scrutiny will reveal that Jesus is saying that what God wills in heaven must be going on in this earth as well. It is clearly God's idea for us to pray for things to be here, as they are in heaven. Thy will be done on earth, as it is in heaven. That is stupendous. Therefore, it is God's order that we pray that whatever is going on earth must align with His heavenly will. And, since there are no persons in heaven with cancer, should there be people with cancer here on earth? My view is to speak to the cancer or diabetes or whatever it is and say, "Spirit of cancer or diabetes or infirmity, since you do not exist in heaven, you are not allowed to exist here in my body. You must be here illegally, and I forbid you to establish yourself in my body." Then bind that spirit of infirmity to the Word of God in the name of Jesus, who declares that you have authority and power over Satan and all his power, and nothing shall, by any means, hurt you (Luke 10:19). Ask the Holy Spirit to enlighten you on that. I am already deeply convinced about that. Let all unwelcome spirits be removed from my body including spirit of cancer, diabetes, high blood pressure, and any spirit of infirmity because they do not exist in heaven, in the name of Jesus. The Apostle Paul reminds us that our bodies are temples and only the Spirit of God is allowed there (1 Corinthians 3:16).

Some sincere Christians may argue that cancer or diabetes may be God's will for some people. And I acknowledge their sincerity but find it difficult to respect such views because they are confuted by Scripture, which says in 3 John 1:2, "Beloved I wish above *all* things that thou mayest prosper and be in good health even as thy soul prospereth."

Cancer or diabetes does not constitute good health. Nor are they part of the abundant life that Jesus promised.

In everything, give thanks for this is the will of God in Christ Jesus concerning you. Importantly, you cannot do the will of God without a robust personal relationship with the Holy Spirit. Nor is it feasible to be sincere in your worship of God without a strong desire to do the will of God. Jesus associated His kinship with doing the will of God when He said, "Whoever shall do the will of my father which is in heaven, the same is my brother, and sister, and mother" (Matthew 12:50). In addition, one of the lessons we learn from Job's life and the greatest glory we can give God is to submit to His will. Job said, "The Lord gave, and the Lord hath taken away: blessed be the name of the Lord" (Job 1:21). When you submit to God's will, then you ask Him to empower you with His Spirit to do His will.

In the morning, you cannot declare that you want the Holy Spirit to take control of your life if you do not also want His will to be done in your life and on earth. And to yield to God's will is not as easy as it sounds. It is a will that is different from ours. However, God's will is another way of expressing His love towards us. No evil purpose can subvert the will of God because it is His plan for my life and yours, a plan that He conceived before the foundation of the world.

Furthermore, God's will cannot be done on earth without His Power to execute that will. That power is indispensable for the fulfillment of His will. Believe me, if there is one petition that needs to be repeated every day, it is, "Let thy will be done on earth as it is in heaven." When the Angel Gabriel announced to Mary that she had been chosen to be the mother of the Son of God, she said, "Be it unto me according to your word" (Luke 1:38). All Mary was saying was, "Let your will be done." We, too, can repeat that sentiment when we come across a promise by saying what Mary said, "Be it unto me according to your word" (Luke 1:38).

"In everything give thanks for this is the will of God in Christ Jesus concerning you" (1 Thessalonians 5:18). If you are unwilling to give thanks for anything and everything going on in your life, you are out of the will of God during life. I would think so. The reason is that Jesus is more than adequate in any challenge that you may be facing. So that to give thanks in advance is to assert that you know that He is in control and has the last Word. So why worry? Just give thanks.

It is a blessing to know that you are in the will of God. Solomon says, "In all thy ways acknowledge Him, and He shall direct thy paths" (Proverbs 3:6). In all matters, small and large, consult Him and let Him be the one to control you. In Ephesians 5:15–18, Paul says that we "should not be foolish to understand what the Lord's will is." And in chapter 6, verse 6, he says, "doing the will of God from the heart." It is another way of saying that I have surrendered and placed my entire life at the Lord's disposal. God's will can only be done if you are committed to him 100 percent (The *all* or *nothing principle*). Jesus was committed to His Father 100 percent that is why He was able to say, "My meat is to do the will of Him that sent me and to finish His work" (John 4:34). However, it does not imply that since you are doing the will of God from the heart, there will be no untoward circumstances coming your way. It does mean that you expose all your challenges to Him and give Him thanks in all things. Jesus gave us this assurance: "Be of good cheer, I have overcome the world" (John: 16:33). Be of good cheer. We should not forget to be of good cheer. It was not an option but a command from our Lord and Savior Jesus Christ of Nazareth. Paul told those in the boat with him, "Wherefore Sirs, be of good cheer for I believe God, that it shall be even as it was told me" (Acts 27:25). Be of good cheer.

John says, "This is the boldness or confidence that we have toward Him, that, if we ask anything according to His will, He hears us. And if we know that He hears us, whatever we ask, we know that we have the petitions that we ask of Him" (1 John 5:14–15). The truth of the matter is that God reveals His will in His Word. Take the time and trouble to find out the will of God in His Word. Examine the promises of God and see whether they apply to your circumstance and present them to Him. Praying according to what God has promised in His Word is praying in God's will. *Plead His promises to Him.* "Do as thou has said in your Word" is another way of saying it. David said, "Thou art God and hast promised this good thing to thy servant" (1 Chronicles 17:26).

But the certainty of their fulfillment rests in the one who made them and bound Himself to them. From this understanding, I came up with one of my definitions of prayer: prayer is talking *to God about God.*

The Word of God is God (John 1:1), and the greater your confidence in His Word, the more fulfilling your prayer life will be. *Have faith in God's Word.* Jesus made it very clear that God's will was the priority in His mission when He said, "Father, if thou be willing, remove this cup from me: nevertheless, not my will, but thine, be done" (Luke 22:42). Prayer reveals the choice that is inherent in our walk with God. It also means that we all have our wills separate from God's will. That is why it is vital to seek God's will whenever you are about to make a decision that would impact your life and the life of your family, your church family, your work environment, and everyone directly or indirectly affiliated to you. That is the irony. Everything we do affects lots of other people. That is why you and I must seek God's will. Your will turns your back on God. Saul, the first king of Israel, followed his own will instead of God's will. And look at what happened (1 Samuel 13:13–14). Here you find that doing God's will and keeping His commandments are fungible. Food for thought.

It is essential to know and pray for God's will in any matter. We can accomplish it in two ways: *First, you must detach yourself from the circumstances you face so that they do not become the criterion you use to make your decisions. Second, and more importantly, you must resist and forego the temptation of acting with pride (pride is the worship of self) because pride is the greatest threat to answered prayer. In Psalm 9:12b, it says, "He forgets not the cry of the humble."* You are reading this book because of God's will. You are alive because of God's will. Everything we do is part of His will for our lives. However, you cannot do God's will unless you also have an ongoing, salubrious relationship with Him.

I would like to conclude this chapter on prayer and the will of God by stating that the Holy Spirit has everything to do with prayer. *Prayer is impossible without the Holy Spirit. Consult and cultivate the habit of inviting Him in every challenge as you pray, and do not rely on your* prayers, but depend on the God who hears and answers prayers (Psalm 65:2). That is who we need to know more than anything else. *Doing His will is accepting what He wants in your life, for your life, in the first place. Isn't that something? "It is God which worketh in you both to will and to do of His good pleasure" (Philippians 2:13).*

Hymn:

Day by Day
Day by day and with each passing moment,
Strength, I find to meet my trials here;
Trusting in my father's wise bestowment,
I've no cause for worry or for fear.
He whose heart is kind be yond all measure
Gives unto each day what He deems best.
Lovingly, it's part of pain and pleasure,
Mingling toil with peace and rest.

CHAPTER 3
Prayer and Praise

Praise is *the sine qua non* for a prayer warrior. However, I must state at the outset that the foundation of praise is that God reigns and is sovereign and is in complete control of the world.

"From the rising of the sun unto the going down of the same, the Lord's name is to be praised" (Psalm 113:3). "Let everything that has breath praise the Lord" (Psalm 150:6). As you can see, the command is universal. Nevertheless, it takes an entirely different meaning for a prayer warrior because their objective is to create a milieu where God's presence takes complete control of the situation. The powers of darkness are allergic to praises to God. They hate praise. The devil and all his demons are terrified by praise of the Almighty God. Praise makes the enemy powerless and makes the point loud and clear that God has the last Word and is in complete control of all situations. When we praise God, we confess that He reigns over all His creation. *In praise, we are saying that our God has the capacity and ability to rule and overrule all things, bring and bend all things, and showcase His will in the matter. That is why it is always almost impossible to praise God and worry simultaneously. To do so is to betray a defective and inadequate perspective about God.* Praising God in any situation is a reflection of an attitude, and I might add, a necessary view that leads to a correct understanding of our God.

Prayer warriors recognize that when they engage in praise, they ask God to come and take the glory for whatever the challenge may be. Remember Paul and Silas in Acts 16? Scripture states that they prayed and sang praises to God. Prayer and praise are inextricably linked. However, in the end, God received all the glory because a whole family accepted Jesus, and one family depopulated hell. There is no middle ground. Either you are following God, or you are not. He inhabits the praises of His people. In other words, He likes to hear His people praise

His name. "Let them praise the name of the Lord: for His name alone is excellent; his glory is above the earth and heaven" (Psalm 148:13). To praise God in prayer, you must have reached a point in your experience where your heart is made up or fixed (Psalm 57:7).

In addition, people who have understood the concept of praise also have this growing awareness and disposition *that the unseen world interacts and interplays with the seen world, and praise defeats the enemy whom we cannot see at all times in the unseen world.* Remember Elisha and his servant who could not see the chariots of God on their side? Elisha had to pray for God to open his eyes to the unseen world. Praise also brings God to the scene as the sovereign God.

Without peace with God, it is impossible to praise God. In addition, Scripture states that He has given us everything that pertains to life and godliness. Therefore, it makes sense that you have the peace that you will need to praise God for whatever challenges you may be going through. Remember that He is the God of peace. Paul says in Romans 16:20, "And the God of peace shall bruise Satan *under your feet* shortly. The grace of our Lord Jesus Christ be with you. Amen." That should be a new and remarkable discovery for you because it was for me. Satan is under your feet and has been placed there by the God of peace. Also, do well to examine Psalm 8:4–6.

Mark 4:35–41 has one great illustration about peace and praise. (I assume that you will read this portion of Scripture). The Bible says that it was such a violent storm that induced panic among the disciples. Nevertheless, Jesus was peaceful probably because He is the prince of peace.

Praising God in any circumstance is one of the secrets of power and confidence with the God who answers prayers. The Bible says God Inhabits the praises of his people (Psalm 22:3). When Jehoshaphat learned that belligerent nations were advancing towards Judah, his first instinct was fear. However, after he regrouped his thoughts, he prayed *and expressed his helplessness to God.* It is worthwhile to carefully examine 2 Chronicles 20 that recounts a perfect example of effective prayers, *reminding God of your helplessness in any situation and reminding yourself that He is the Almighty God with whom nothing is impossible.* When they started praising God, He came down to the scene and discomfited the enemies of Judah. Discover this strategy if you have not yet done so. *Praising*

God puts the enemy to flight. Praise is your way of saying that the battle is not yours but His if you let Him (Exodus 14:14). How do you praise God, and for what do you praise Him? Do you praise Him because he does wondrous things? Or because He sacrificed His only Son for you and me, and he is coming again for us? Do you or are you praising Him for His greatness, for His power, for His majesty, goodness, indulgent mercy, faithfulness, or for His Glory? Do you praise and thank Him for supplying your daily needs, for His favor and the power in His name? Or do you praise Him because He is God and the only true God? Or are you praising Him for His voice? See Isaiah 30:31. You must make that choice because you are the only one who knows what He has done for you and is doing for you. I am told that there is a difference between praising God and thanking Him. We praise Him for who He is and thank Him for what He does for us daily. I suggest that you do both because the difference is artificial and may even be superficial.

People who praise God are people who know Him. Praise is so critical to prayer warriors, and that is where they begin their conversation with God. Let praise become a lifestyle. All prayers about challenges should start with praise to God about the challenge. Always make sure that your garment is pure and white and that your head does not lack oil at any time (Ecclesiastes 9:8).

Nevertheless, praise is not a magic wand. We must confess our sins, avoid bitterness, and learn to forgive. You must be right with your fellowmen to prevail as a prayer warrior. Holding grudges and grievances against people who have done you wrong disqualifies you entirely as a prayer warrior no matter whether you are a pastor, a leader in the church, or a prayer coordinator. Instead, exchange your life for His, live for Christ daily, and dethrone self. Enthrone Christ and reckon yourself dead daily to self and sin and alive to God. Put on the Lord Jesus. If you strongly feel that you are guilty of violating Malachi 2:10 or that you have added Christ to your life without subtracting sin, ask the Holy Spirit to possess you so that who you are in Christ will determine your actions and thoughts. Because it is who you are that determines what you do and how you act. *To be a prayer warrior, you must think and act like Jesus. And believe it or not, that is the definition of a true Christian. Someone who has been baptized in the name of God the Father, God the Son, and God the Holy Ghost, and who thinks and acts like Jesus.* That is the summary of His only sermon found in the gospel of Matthew chapters 5, 6, and 7: *Act like a child of God.* A prayer warrior does not engage in known sin and expect praise to bring honor to God and improve their prayer life. For a thorough understanding of the incompatibility of sin and the fulfillment of their mission, prayer warriors should read 1 John 3:9.

Our God answers prayers in ways that contribute to His plans and purposes and in harmony with His will. (1 John 5:14–15). We must praise Him from the rising of the sun to the going down of the same. However, the Holy Spirit has a vital role to play in initiating praise to God in your experience. *It is the case, and always the case, that when we praise God in times when everything is contrary to our wellbeing or happiness, then we discover that the worst things are not always the last things with God. Why? Because all things work together for good to them who love God (Romans 8:28). Finally, let me say that no component of a building is as critical to its stability as its foundation. Praise is the foundation of prayer especially when we praise Him before the deliverance. In 2 Chronicles 20, Jehoshaphat and the people praised God before their victory, and the children of Israel praised God only after escaping from Pharaoh's army (Exodus 15:1). The difference is remarkable and critical. Praise is faith in action.*

Hymn:

> *Trust and obey:*
> *When we walk with the Lord*
> *In the light of His Word,*
> *What a glory He sheds on our way!*
> *While we do His good will,*
> *He abides with us still,*
> *And with all who will trust and obey.*
> *Refrain*
> *Trust and obey, for there's no other way to be happy*
> *   in Jesus, but to trust and obey.*

CHAPTER 4
Prayer and Faith

Whatever *your* faith says God is, He will be. In other words, what God does for you is determined by what He is to you. Faith is a mystery that a prayer warrior must thoroughly understand. Faith is receiving and welcoming that in which you believe. You make it your own. And mixing the Word of God with faith in His faithfulness (which abides forever) tends to reveal the truth that all things are possible with God. God answers our prayers based on our faith, and faith is a divine gift to all believers. Faith is constantly preoccupied with God, who is invisible (Hebrews 11:27). For a prayer warrior, faith and fear cannot coexist. Prayer warriors who believe that the Lord is all-powerful become fearless (Psalm 46:1–2). Jesus told two blind minds, "According to your faith, let it be to you" (Matthew 9:29). Faith is the currency in heaven. The bigger our view of God, the bigger He can be in our lives. If your God is small, He will be small in our lives. Furthermore, faith in God is the only basis for righteousness. So as a prayer warrior, you are right with God through faith. However, because God is sovereign, faith is not always confidence in the outcome of our expectations. Although that is integral to our faith in God. Instead, faith is the confidence in both the power of God to do anything, but also the wisdom of God to do only the best thing that will bring glory to His name (1 Corinthians 1:24). It is confidence in the *character of God*, that *He* is righteous in all His ways. The three Hebrew boys had confidence in the character of God not necessarily the outcome. The Bible teaches us that God is a rewarder of those who diligently seek Him. You cannot seek Him if you do not believe or have Faith in Him. Listen to Jesus "Therefore I say unto you, what things soever ye desire, when you pray, believe that ye receive them, and ye shall have them" (Mark 11:24). Faith is above circumstances, and it triumphs over *all* difficulties. Faith is the staff that we walk with here on earth because we are enjoined to walk by faith; and to live by faith (2 Corinthians 5:7; Romans 1:17).

Believers who live by faith understand that there are two realms of reality, the unseen and the seen. But they also know that it is the unseen realm that controls the seen. To live by faith is to live in harmony with the Word of God. It is occasionally a challenge for some believers because they have not fully understood *that faith concerns itself with facts about the invisible. The promises of God are, in a real sense, facts about the invisible wrapped up and clothed in words.* The Bible is noticeably clear that without faith, it is impossible to please God. Please Him we must. Jesus's mission was to do God's will, which is another way of pleasing God. And in keeping with His *modus operandi*, God gave Jesus the Spirit that enabled Him to do only those things that would please Him (Isaiah 11:2). Whatever God wants you to do, He gives you everything that would enable you to do it. "He has given you and me everything that pertains to life and godliness" (2 Peter 1:3). He has also given you a measure of faith that you need to utilize daily.

In healthcare policy, there was a raging debate about the utilization of health services by those with health insurance. In other words, do people with health insurance utilize more health services and, therefore, increase healthcare costs? The drive to contain healthcare costs tends to increase scrutiny about utilization of healthcare services. Patients go to their doctor or provider even with ailments that do not require a doctor's visit. The debate is still ongoing. The idea is to discourage the excessive use of health services to contain costs. Faith, however, is different. I encourage you to utilize it as often as necessary and on everything that bothers you. We should remember that a little thing is a little thing, but faithfulness in little things is a great thing. That is pretty much how faith operates. Always exercise your faith in God as the situation calls for.

Faith is such a mysterious concept that only God sees it. Unless it manifests itself through your actions, it will escape your spouse, your pastor, or anyone else who encounters you. He told Peter that Satan's desire was to sift and destroy him. But He said, "I have prayed for you that your faith fail not."

Jesus was stressing the importance of faith in the life of a believer. The irony is that Satan works tenaciously to disconnect you from your prayer life, knowing fully well that it has the potential to destroy your faith. A group of prayer warriors brought their friend who was sick to Jesus, and because of the crowd, they had to go through the roof. The Bible says Jesus saw their faith. On numerous occasions, people received their healing because of the quality of their faith. The woman with the issue of blood is a glaring example. In Matthew chapter 8, the centurion said, "Only speak a word." Faith is so important to God and to a prayer warrior that it is the secret weapon in the life of anyone determined to engage the enemy in spiritual warfare. Spurgeon quipped that a believer who prays and entertains doubts that his prayer would be answered is worse than an atheist.

So what is faith? The Bible says, "Faith is the substance of things hoped for, the evidence of things not seen" (Hebrews 11:1). So what does that mean? It may mean different things to different people. Here is what it means to me: Faith is taking *God's Word and acting on it*, period. In Luke 5:5, Peter said to Jesus, "We have toiled all night and caught nothing: *nevertheless, at thy word.*" And the catch was miraculous because he took God's Word at face value. I am referring here to God's promises. My study Bible has all the promises of God highlighted, and that is because I live in the promises of God. For Jesus Himself said, "Man shall not live by bread alone but by every word that proceeds out of the mouth of God" (Matthew 4:4). Faith is living daily by God's Word regardless of the circumstances you may be facing. That is because God's Word is God (John 1:1) and because He cannot fail you, neither can His Word. In another sense, it is calling those things that are not as if they are (Romans 4:17).

Remember what the Scripture says, "Evidence of things not seen." But I must hasten to add that prayer warriors know or, at least, should know the difference between faith and presumption, and I will leave it there. Faith, and I mean faith in God and His Word, operates and depends on your knowledge of God through the Holy Ghost. Do you know and believe in His great and precious promises? Knowledge of His character or attributes tends to increase and strengthen your confidence in Him. Faith in God allows you to live by His promises and brings you closer to God. This closeness translates into pleasing Him because without faith, we cannot please Him. But with faith, our life becomes pleasing to Him, and you become overly sensitive to sin. Hebrews 11:5 reminds us that before his translation, Enoch pleased God.

Pleasing God means, among other things, that your friendship and fellowship with the Holy Spirit adds immeasurable value to your life in ways that make you want to be always in His presence. And the more you are in His presence, the more the things of the world lose their hold and grip on you. Even watching television becomes unattractive to you. In Psalm 16:11, the Psalmist says in part, "In His presence is fullness of joy, at Thy right hand there are pleasures forevermore. The French monk, Brother Lawrence, wrote a popular book *Practicing His Presence*. It may sound paradoxical that the more you are in His presence, the more your thirst for Him heightens. The joy of His presence becomes your strength. At this point, you have no choice but to invite others to come and *"taste and see that the Lord is good." Nobody can experience this for you. Jesus wants to live His life in you through His Spirit, and when that happens, you will begin to participate in His divine nature.* That is Christianity at its best. According to Apostle Paul, when that happens, He begins to pray through us for we do not know how to pray and what to pray for (Romans 8:26).

Several years ago, in the Southwest province of Cameroon where I was born, I said to myself, "I will go to the United States for further studies." I was professing to myself the same way the woman with the issue of blood for twelve years confessed to her Spirit. She said, "If I but touch the hem of His garment, I will be healed." She was healed, and I came to the United States. For me, confessing God's Word to the Spirit that dwells in me is faith. That is because the Spirit of God that dwells in you and me always responds to your confession of God's Word. "By thy words, thou shall be justified, and by thy words, thou shall be condemned" (Matthew 12:37). The power of life and death are in the tongue (Proverbs 18:21). "No weapon formed against me, or you shall prosper." Do you believe that? It does not say no weapon will be formed against you. Rather, it says that no weapon formed against you *shall prosper.* The promise is that it shall not prosper. These signs shall follow those who believe. Do you believe that promise from Jesus? Acting on God's Word or promises is faith. There is a sense in which faith is the victory and the answer to every challenge. Those who believe in the reliability of God's character trust in the promise that says, "All things work together for good to those who love God and to those who are called according to His purpose" (Romans 8:28).

They are not circumstance-driven believers. They are Christ-directed believers. They believe that in *all* things, Christ is still in control. Do not let the assault of negative circumstances determine your response to His faithfulness. *Great faith is experienced when you place yourself at His disposal or when you cast all your cares upon Him. Did you know that miracles are a reward of faith? Faith in God and His word places you in miracle territory.*

Let me conclude this chapter on faith and prayer with an object lesson on faith by Jesus Himself, who is the way and the truth and the life. I would rather listen to Jesus, who is the truth, teach the truth about faith than anyone else. In the teaching about the fig tree in Matthew 21:21, Jesus says, *"If you have faith and do not doubt*, but believe, you can speak to your mountains, and they will obey you." Let Jesus speak for Himself, "I will tell you the truth. If you have faith and do not doubt, not only can you do what was done to the fig tree, but also you and me (believers) can say to this mountain, go throw yourself into the sea, and it will be done." Faith mainly involves speaking God's promises over your challenges with a strong belief that what God has promised in His Word cannot fail. It is amazing. For example, "the Lord shall preserve my going out and my coming in from this time forth and even forevermore" (Psalm 121:8). Or "Let my mouth be filled with Thy praise and with Thy honor all day" (Psalm 71:8). Or "For thou hast been a shelter for me, and a strong tower from the enemy" (Psalm 61:3). "Deal bountifully with thy servant that I may live and keep thy word" (Psalm 119:17). In thy name shall they rejoice all day; and in thy righteousness shall they be exalted (Psalm 89:16). You must conclude that it contributes to the glory of God the Father, the Son, and the Holy Ghost, amen and amen. Say this aloud as you leave your house, and *believe it with all your heart.* That is the recommendation from Jesus. He says you can say. *While it is true that faith is a gift to us, our response to God is to trust His character. The laborers (in the parable of the laborers) who did not make any bargain and worked just for two hours but trusted in the Landowner's character and promise when He said, "You will receive what is right," were surprised at the generosity of God. He paid them not what they deserved but what they needed. God is delighted when we trust Him with all our hearts and minds. "So, my trust in God is the highest expression of my love for Him. However, even your trust in Him is* not self-initiated. You have to say, "Lord, I want to trust you more than I do now. We must depend on God for everything." Jesus announced in His Word that without Him, we cannot do anything (John 15:5), and that includes and involves trusting Him. Did you know that little acts of trust make larger room for God? As a prayer warrior, you must resign yourself to the fact that we are dependent creatures. Since Jesus is our example in everything, the question is, do you have the faith of Jesus? And I do not mean faith in Jesus, but the faith of Jesus. Jesus depended on His Father's power for everything that He accomplished. I encourage you to ask the Holy Spirit for the faith of Jesus, who depended implicitly on His Father's power. We, too, can rely on the power of the Holy Spirit for everything. However, you must ask for the faith of Jesus. And the truth is that every sincere prayer from the heart is answered. There is no asking without receiving and no receiving without asking. Amen.

Hymn:

"'Tis So Sweet to Trust in Jesus:
'Tis So Sweet to trust in Jesus,
Just to take Him at His Word.
Just to rest upon His promise,
Just to know, 'Thus saith the Lord.'"
Refrain
Jesus, Jesus, how I trust Him.
How I've proved Him o'er and o'er!
Jesus, Jesus, precious Jesus!
O for grace to trust Him more!

CHAPTER 5
Prayer and Witnessing

If the Bible message is credible, and I know that it is, then it is imperative to acknowledge the importance of the resurrection in its entirety.

We are all here because Jesus resurrected from the grave, and there would be nothing called Christianity if Jesus did not emerge from the grave.

Why is this important? It is crucial because you cannot *believe* in the resurrection without also believing in the Second Coming of Jesus, the Anointed One, for that is what Christ means. They are intricately linked.

And if you believe in the Second Coming of Jesus Christ, then you must not only be actively waiting for *Him*, but your dominant desire becomes witnessing for Him that He is God (Isaiah 43:12).

Enter prayer warriors:

Who are these people waiting for Jesus, and how are they called? They are called witnesses. They believe that prayer undergirds witnessing and witnessing cultivates a culture of absolute and undeviating dependence on the Holy Spirit. In the tenth chapter of Acts, Peter told Cornelius and the Gentiles he was instructed to visit in Caesarea that when Jesus resurrected, He commissioned people to be witnesses (verse 41). *If you are a prayer warrior witnessing for Jesus, you have a divinely appointed mission and are considered a high privileged Christian.* Prayer warriors are witnesses of God's power to change lives. Their mandate is to prepare the world for the Second Coming of Jesus Christ. Their testimony is about the transformation of lives by God's power. That is indeed their mission statement. They exist to prepare the world for the Second Coming of Jesus Christ through prayer. But the focal point of their activities is persuading men, women, boys, and girls to be reconciled to God. Although witnessing is the responsibility of every Christian, prayer warriors take this assignment to a different level. The few prayer warriors with whom I come in contact with recognize the imminence of the end of time. They understand that time, and the things of time will end sooner than we expect. In these last days, there seems to be a devaluation of our values as Christians. Right is becoming wrong, and wrong is becoming right. Even the very elect is compromising with sin and all the dangers associated with it. *But the power of prayer warriors resides in their consecrated prayer life.* And believe it or not, the beauty of a consecrated prayer life can never be more revealed than in your hourly and daily walk with God. They take seriously the breathtaking affirmation from Jesus when He says, "If ye abide in me, and my words abide in you, you shall ask what you desire, and it shall be done for you" (John 15:7). If you meet the conditions, you will not have to do anything, but it shall be done for you, and that is answered prayer. *The keynote in that text is that it shall be done for you.* They know that in prayer, it is their life that prays (see Daniel 11:32b). "The prayer of a righteous man *is powerful and effective*" (James 5:16). They pray for the presence of God to accompany them to reach unsaved souls for the Lord Jesus. They go to God asking for favor with the people and access to their hearts. Only God can do that, and He did it with Lydia (Acts 16:14), which means they purpose in their hearts to get connected with the power of the Holy Ghost always and to walk in the Spirit's power (Galatians 5:16). *Their chief and principal concern revolves around unsaved souls.* They do not look at them as homosexuals, transgender people, lesbians, and atheists, *but as souls to be saved.* Why? Because all souls belong to God (Ezekiel 18:4). They are responding to Jesus when He says go and compel them to come. They reckon and recognize, more than most, that Jesus taught that it is His Father who draws people to Himself. "Nobody can come to me except my father who sent me draws him" (John 6:44). They (prayer warriors) are just channels, vessels, and ambassadors for that purpose.

Furthermore, the few that I know do not pray long prayers. In artless and pristine simplicity and from their hearts, they implore God to go before them and prepare the hearts of the people to whom He is directing them. *It must be noted and stressed that witnessing points people to Jesus who knows what they need. And this can be accomplished only through the power of the Holy Spirit.* That is why you hear testimonies like, "I was not planning to come to this clinic today, but now I know why I came here so you could tell me what you just told me. Thank you so much." Then the prayer warrior, careful not to take credit (because that can be very deadly), says, "Let us praise the Lord for it is His doing." Then a prayer of thanksgiving is offered to God. *Witnessing to the world about the love of Jesus is where the church needs the Holy Spirit the most because the raison d'être of the church is tied to witnessing.*

The text that comes to mind that underscores witnessing for a prayer warrior is found in Acts 1:8. It says, "You shall receive power after the Holy Ghost is come upon you, and ye shall be witnesses unto me both in Jerusalem and in all Judea and Samaria and unto the uttermost parts of the earth." Interestingly, witnessing begins or should begin at home. That is the hardest or most challenging kind of witnessing. This is important for many reasons. Prominent among them is that the transformation becomes evident to those who know you best. As a result, they, too, are impacted by your miraculous change through Jesus Christ. That is the underlying motive. The story of the man with the unclean spirit in Mark 5:14–20 is very instructive. In verse 20, it says *all men* did marvel. They marveled because of the change that had been wrought and that they could now see in his life. (*All men except none.*) A man or woman who used to smoke or drink and is now a witness for Christ and no longer drinks or smokes is a compelling witness. They do not tell you about their denominations *and their doctrines*. All they know is that they have been restored to sanity by the power of Jesus, and that is all they talk about *Jesus.* The reason is that witnessing is about Jesus, nothing more, nothing less, and nothing else. *Listen to what happens to prayer warriors, "And the hand of the Lord was with them; and a great number believed and turned to the Lord" (Acts 11:21).*

I cannot pass this opportunity to share my testimony of how I quit smoking several years ago. This experience taught me that prayer is a tangible expression of your dependence on God. It is honest communication from your heart to God. *I learned that he who prays from the heart is talking to God.* All my efforts to quit had failed woefully, and I prayed and said, "Holy Father, I desire to quit smoking. Help me in Jesus's name." It was a miracle because after four days, I quit smoking. It is now thirty years since I quit smoking. Everyone was surprised at the change that took place within me. God was actually doing what He promised in His word when He said that He will give us the desires of our heart (Psalm 37:4). Not wicked desires.

A careful reading reveals that the power for witnessing is not about your *denominations or doctrines*, as we are wont to do. *Doctrines do not save; it is Jesus who saves.* It clearly says, "You shall be witnesses unto me." The power is also not to defend God as apologists. God is eminently able to defend Himself. It is also not to point out the faults of the Jehovah's Witnesses or to chastise the Catholic church, Sunday worshippers, Sabbath worshippers, or Mormons, and other Christians. It is not about exhibiting your ability to quote Scripture. *Anytime prayer warriors talk and extol their denominations, there is bound to be a conflict because, at that point, Jesus has ceased to be the main issue.* However, the moment you resume talking about Jesus, there is a strong likelihood that there will be a confluence of agreement, and when that happens, *Jesus* takes control of the encounter. *Do not forget that Jesus is the protagonist in witnessing, not our denominations, as crucial as that may be to us.* Jesus is the paragon, and we are not. Prayer warriors are at their best when they are uplifting the name of Jesus. They are at their worst when they criticize other Christians or denominations. The names of our various denominations cannot save us. Only the name of Jesus can. Scripture says, "There is no other name under heaven given among men whereby we must be saved" (Acts 4:12). Any prayer warrior who misses or misreads this point has disqualified himself or herself as a faithful prayer warrior. We do not go into the community, telling people about our denominations and how our denominations can save them. Instead, we tell them about Jesus.

Most Christians have not understood clearly (I think) that there will be no denominations in heaven. The only characteristic that would identify the saved would be "the redeemed." Please, not members of the Redeemed church, but those who have been redeemed from the hand of the enemy. Those who have overcome the enemy through the blood of the Lamb and by the Word of their testimonies (Revelation 12:11).

I encountered a man who claimed that I hit his car, although that was not the case. I was backing up and accidently touched his right front tire. He came out of his car and angrily accused me of hitting his car. There was no dent on any part of his car except some mud on his tire. After a few minutes of squabbling back and forth, we both agreed that there was no need to call the police because the contact was not on any part of his car except his tire. I invited him for a brief prayer. He initially refused to pray and insisted on knowing my denomination. When I informed him that I was a practicing Seventh-day Adventist, he said he could not pray with me because SDAs are not Christians. But then he suggested that he should be the only one to pray. In the end, he prayed and agreed that I should pray as well. So, the cacophonies that we see and hear about our denominational differences or superiority and the attendant ethnocentricity are a nonissue and a profound misunderstanding. The disciples came to Jesus and gossiped about people performing miracles and were not members of His circle.

Jesus's response has been ignored by those who uplift their congregations or denominations. He said those who are not against us are with and for us. Peter told the centurion that God is not a respecter of persons, but He accepts anyone who fears Him and lives a righteous life. The context of that dialogue between Peter and the Gentiles supports the idea that our denominations are not the central issue in witnessing. The primary and overriding point is, has always been, and will continue to be Jesus. In the Gospel of John, the blind man says, "Now we know that God heareth not sinners: but if any man be a worshipper of God, and doeth His will, him He heareth" (John 9:31). Any denomination that uplifts Jesus is doing the right thing. And whether they worship on the Sabbath or Sunday is not for us to judge. The Bible tells us that a servant falls or stands only before his Master (Romans 14:4). Jesus is the Master. Whether their teaching on the state of the dead is not in accordance with Scripture is for God to judge. We are not their masters to judge who is right and who is wrong. We do not receive worship. Therefore, it is beyond our ken to determine which congregation or denomination worships in truth and in Spirit. When Jesus met the woman at the well in the book of John, she, in all sincerity, and I believe she was sincere, tried to introduce and induce the idea of denominational worship. The teaching that Jesus announced to her many centuries earlier is still applicable to us in the twenty-first century. Jesus taught that worship done in Spirit and in truth is the only acceptable form of worship. Let me say here that the truth is not Jesus; rather, Jesus is the truth. I have heard people say we have the truth, we preach the truth, like no other church. But the truth about this truth is that you can have the truth and not have Jesus. Importantly, you cannot have Jesus without also having the truth. Let us ask for the Spirit of truth to guide us. *Let it be known that the compassion, love, goodness, and grace of God is not tied and will never be tied to any religious tradition or denomination.* We must bring a balanced voice that uplifts Jesus, not the misinformation and misstatements of the Popes over the years. Criticizing others does not lead any soul to Jesus. And no congregation or denomination could and should claim ownership to be doing it the right way. Although you could argue that there must be a right and wrong way because that is in the nature of things. In Psalm 11:7, the Bible makes it limpidly clear that "upright men will see His face." Not upright men in any denomination. I cannot stress enough that my chief aim has been to exalt the Holy Spirit in our prayer lives. Remember this, "A true witness delivereth souls" (Proverbs 14:25).

That is why the title of this book is *facts* and *interpretations*. The facts in the Bible can be interpreted correctly, only as you develop and cultivate a genuine relationship with the Holy Spirit. Jesus said the Holy Spirit will teach you *all* things.

Hymn:

> *Rescue the perishing,*
> *Rescue the perishing,*
> *Care for the dying.*
> *Snatch them in pity from sin and the grave.*
> *Weep o'er the erring one,*
> *Lift up the fallen,*
> *Tell them of Jesus, the mighty to save.*
> *Refrain*
> *Rescue the perishing,*
> *Care for the dying.*
> *Jesus is Merciful,*
> *Jesus will save.*

CHAPTER 6
Prayer and the Sovereignty of God

It is indisputable that, as the Creator, God is sovereign. "O Lord, I know that the way of man is not in himself: It is not in man that walketh to direct his steps" (Jeremiah 10:23). As you may recall, Jeremiah said this when his people were going into Babylonian captivity. The prophet is expressing what he knows about the sovereignty of God. He is intimating that despite this sad situation, God is still in control and that their captivity was not under the control of Nebuchadnezzar. He is saying the God, who rules and overrules, works according to His eternal purposes. In other words, God is the one who initiates and regulates all things for His eternal purposes.

Furthermore, in Proverbs 20:24, the Bible says that "Man's goings are of the Lord, how can a man then understand his own way?" Or Psalm 24:1, "The earth is the Lord's and the fullness thereof; the world and they that dwell therein."

Nowhere is our Creator-creature relationship more pronounced as in our concept of God's sovereignty and prayer. As we pray, we must also know and remember that God knows the end from the beginning and has all the answers before we even start praying because the Word of God says, "He worketh all things after the counsel of His own will" (Ephesians 1:11). Prayer warriors must know that our prayers do not inform God of what He does not already know. "For your Father knows what things you have in need of before ye ask Him" (Matthew 6:8). That is because before God created the world, He had a plan and a purpose that nobody can thwart (Job 42:2), so that when we pray, we are saying, "Hasten your plans and purposes for your people. Let thy will be done." We are not saying do what is outside your plans and purposes. However, He can do anything even if it is beyond His purposes, and nobody can question Him (Psalm 135:5–6). In the epistle to the Romans, the Apostle Paul says, "For He says to Moses, I will have mercy on whom I will have mercy and will have compassion on whom I will have compassion so then it is not of him that willeth nor of him that runneth, but of God that showeth mercy" (Romans 9:15–16; see also Jeremiah 29:11). That is why I stated earlier that, "Your will be done on earth as it is in heaven" is the greatest prayer that you and I can pray every day of our lives, and it will never be considered monotonous. The prayer "Thy will be done on earth as it is in heaven" has been associated with a lot of miracles. That is what we want; that is what He wants, and that is what brings glory to His name. *My understanding is that answered prayer is always on God's terms.*

Even our prayers for the recovery of a dying cancer patient are part of His own eternal will. Whether the patient dies or is healed brings corroboration to our belief in His sovereignty. To be sovereign means that He alone knows all the facts and what He is doing and what is suitable for that family and will bring Him glory, and we do not. That is an important point to consider as a prayer warrior. According to Acts 13:36, David died only after completing the mission assigned to him in this life. *That mission is what we do not know, and only God knows. That is why He alone is God.*

In addition, most Christians have not yet realized that in His mission to reinstate fallen humanity to its original state, Jesus spent about one-third of His time to checkmate Satan and the powers of darkness. He chose prayer as the appointed means to defeat Satan and the forces of darkness. That is why prayer is so vital to a prayer warrior. As Christians, our mission is to participate in weakening and defeating the powers of darkness through prayer. But prayer without a daily study of the Word will not get the job done because the enemy knows the power in the Word. The Word of God is a sword. *A prayer warrior cannot go out there as an ambassador without using his sword: the Word of God. That is how we paralyze the enemy of our souls. Martin Luther wrote the anthem, "A Mighty Fortress is our God."* In the third verse, towards the end, he says, "For Lo his doom is sure, one little word shall fell him." He is correct as far as it goes. It is the Word of God that defeats the devil. Jesus told Satan to get thee behind me, and he complied. How many times have you told Satan to get behind you when he brings up evil thoughts in your mind? Maybe you should start giving people the Word of God. The Lord is your keeper; "no weapon that is formed against you shall prosper" (Isaiah 54:17); "I shall never leave you nor forsake you" (Hebrews 13:5). Your times are in His hands. All those promises that make the enemy of our soul's tremble.

And none of us, if honest, can fail to observe and be impressed with the notion that the early church experienced more victories against and over the powers of darkness than the church of the twenty-first century. The book of Acts presents the history of the early church. Prayer was their battle-axe and weapon of war. They prayed about everything, including boldness to witness. And each time, their prayers were answered because they relied heavily on the power of the Holy Spirit. Regrettably, we do not always remember the lessons of the past. History is more than the path left by the past; it influences the present and potentially shapes the future. We are not using the strategies left for us by the early church.

Concluding this chapter on prayer and the sovereignty of God, we need to ask and answer a crucial question: What is the relationship or what ought to be the relationship between prayer and the sovereignty of God? *We have said that a Sovereign God has power over all His creation, and nothing is beyond His power to achieve.* I think that because He is the Creator and knows what is best for all His people, the only way to sustain this relationship is to say He is God. Let Him do what seems best in His sight for the glory of His name. Whatever He does, our response should be, "Thank you, and we praise you and exalt your name." The Bible admonishes us to give thanks in all things. But where does that lead or leave us? It means that we know who we are and understand who He is. That He is both the Creator and the Redeemer and has all the answers, and we do not.

I have aimed to create a composite portrait of a prayer warrior. They know God, and God knows them. But in knowing God, the prayer warrior does not try to be God. They let God be God in everything. And those who let God be God in everything also pray about *everything*. And that is also made possible by the Holy Spirit as you interact with Him constantly.

Hymn:

Courage Brother
(1) Courage brother, do not stumble though thy path
    be dark as night;
There's a star to guide the humble
Trust in God and do the right.
(7) Some will hate thee, some will love thee
Some will flatter, some will slight
Cease from man, and look above thee,
Trust in God, and do the right.

CHAPTER 7
Secret Prayer

Jesus recommended secret prayer. He said to pray in your closet (secret), and God who sees in secret will reward you openly. The foundation of secret prayer is 1 John 3:22–24. It says, "Whatsoever we ask, we receive of Him because we keep His commandments and do those things that are pleasing in His sight. And this is His commandment that we should believe in the name of His Son, Jesus Christ, and love one another as He gave us commandment. And he that keepeth His commandments dwelleth in Him, and he in Him. And consequently, we know that He abideth in us by the Spirit, which He hath given us."

We stand in the gap for souls and expect a swift response from God because we keep His commandments. We said earlier that God does not respect individuals but respects conditions. God will answer our prayers for souls if we keep His commandments. He says whatsoever we ask, we will receive, and since our preoccupation as prayer warriors is soul winning, we can be sure and assured that God will respond to our prayers for souls. Secret prayer is the beachhead where we launch the attack against the god of this world. Through prayer, we command Satan to release God's people so that they can serve Him. Let me say parenthetically that on our own, it is impossible to keep God's commandments. Our opening text says that God abides in us by the Spirit He has given us. When we yield to God in total surrender, the Holy Spirit exerts full authority to live His life in us. At that point, we will be able to say with Apostle Paul that it is not I but Christ who lives in me, and the life that I now live, I live by the power of Christ in me (Galatians 2:20). *It becomes easier to rebuke impure thoughts (a vice that impacts a good section of Christians); instead of entertaining them, you take them captive through the power of the Holy Ghost.* And pray freely for those who hate and despitefully use you, and that the love of God in your heart deposited by the Holy Spirit begins to manifest Himself in your life. That transformation is possible only as you surrender and deliberately abandon the driver's seat of your life to the Holy Spirit. Keeping the commandments at that point becomes easier "for it is God who works in you both to will and to do for His good pleasure" (Philippians 2:13). It is in secret prayer that we win the battle for souls, and we cry out to God like King David of old when he said, "I will cry out to God Most High, to God who performs *all things* for me" (Psalm 57:2). God wants to perform all things for you and me, not just because He is the Most High God. And indeed, there is no other God greater and bigger and wiser than God, but because he is a God who remembers His covenant to His people.

Furthermore, *all* power belongs to Him, and nobody can challenge Him. There is a sense in which you may ask whether there is a difference between praying and crying out to God out of curiosity. In other words, what does it mean to cry out to God as David is saying that he would do? He says, "I will cry out to God Most High." We know that a child cries to seek attention for a particular need. Are we seeking attention when we cry out to the Lord? I think so wholeheartedly. In times of deep distress and anguish, the only choice we have is to cry out. Scripture says in Psalm 50:15, "Call upon me in the day of trouble; I will deliver you, and you shall glorify me." "When I cry unto thee, then shall mine enemies turn back: this I know for God is for me" (Psalm 56:9). "The righteous cry, and the Lord hears and delivers them out of all their troubles" (Psalm 34:17). "He will fulfill the desire of them that fear Him: He also will hear their cry and will save them" (Psalm 145:19). He forgets not the cry of the humble (Psalm 9:2). He heard the cry of the Israelites when under Egyptian bondage.

(Nehemiah 9:9–11). When they could not find fresh water in the wilderness, He heard and responded to their cry (Exodus 15:25). When Peter was sinking underwater and experienced a temporary bondage of doubt (doubting God is the most severe form of slavery), he cried and said, "Lord, save me," and Jesus rescued him. (Matthew 14:30–31). *Doubting is tantamount to unbelief, and unbelief is also a form bondage (bondage of unbelief) that prevented Jesus from manifesting His power toward His people. The one who doubts has put himself or herself deliberately in a position where they cannot be helped, and that is the worst kind of bondage to be in.* The father who brought his son to Jesus because he was suffering from epilepsy told Jesus to help his unbelief. He said, "I believe help my unbelief." He knew that unbelief is the worst place to find yourself when dealing with Jesus. But the one incident that exemplifies crying out that stands out for me is the blind man in Luke 18:38. The Bible account says he cried out to Jesus, saying, "Jesus, thou son of David have mercy on me." *Your ministry will not make a difference if you are not crying out for souls as a prayer warrior.* Crying out is an expression of your faith in God, and trust in His power and goodness to act on behalf of the souls you are placing before Him. But if you regard iniquity in your heart, the Lord will not hear your cry (Psalm 66:18). That is the bottom line with crying out to the Lord. But the good news is that all who cried out to Him got their requests. So would you. So let us be quick to cry out to God but with sincerity and faith that our God "will fulfill the desire of them that fear him: He also will hear their cry and will save them" (Psalm 145:19). It says He will hear their cry, not that He might, but that indeed He *shall.* Now, that is very reassuring and fulfilling, especially coming from God, the one whose name is the God who hears and answers prayers.

Secret prayer is a place where you unpack everything about your walk with the Lord. You come clean with your foibles. It is a place where you are very transparent with God. You meet with God at that place and time, and no worldly assignment is more important to you. Six times in the book of Exodus, God initiates meeting with His people when He says, "I will meet with you" (Exodus 25:22). In that encounter, intercession for others occupies your praying. In secret prayer, you can pray as long as you want because you are not in any hurry. Your mission and ministry as a prayer warrior takes root in the closet of secret prayer, and ministry is what you do for others in the name of Jesus. At its best, prayer is in the private audience with Jesus.

Furthermore, in secret prayer, we boast about our weaknesses to do our assignments, and that is when we become strong. But secret prayer has to do altogether with the maintenance of the prayer warrior's spiritual communion with his Lord. The everyday tragedy we face as prayer warriors is that we do not take advantage of the precious privilege of secret prayer. *The secret of secret prayer is to pray in secret. The outcome of secret prayer is that you become victorious and fruitful in your service as a prayer warrior when you constantly communicate with heaven for souls.*

Where do we go from here?

I decided to write this book for more than one reason. If you are a born-again Christian (converted Christian), this manual should be in your library. As Christians, we must die daily, take our crosses, and deliberately follow Jesus, the Captain of our salvation. I have met Christians who are considered experts in prayer but who do not pray. Anyone who has encountered the Holy Spirit in their prayer life and understands the concept and power unleashed in prayer can think of themselves as the most secure individual. This manual has been written for them, the most secure Christians. *They are called prayer warriors. These are those who have taken praying for souls not as an avocation but as a vocation. They understand that their lives and their talents belong to God.* Let me say it again, that our talents belong to God, and that is because they came from Him in the first place. And any prayer warrior who acts as though their talent is responsible for the spiritual changes witnessed in the lives of souls they are working with is acting like a mailman claiming credit for ending a war because he delivered the peace documents. *"For a man can receive nothing unless it be given to him from heaven" (John 3:27), including what they lack to fulfill His purposes.*

The second category that will benefit from this manual are those Christians who have discovered that their strength lies in their helplessness as instruments and vessels. They pray and imitate the king of Judah who said, "We do not know what to do, but our eyes are on you."

The third set of Christians are those who want to serve the Lord but have not realized what they want to become. Let them remember that what they want to do for the Lord is all within the possibility of prayer.

Jesus called His disciples and gave them power and authority overall, and I mean all the power of the enemy. This power was made manifest at the cross where Satan was defeated. However, this power only takes center stage in the life of prayer warriors when they mix prayer with fasting. The power that flows and follows from mixing prayer and fasting to reach souls for Christ is still underused and misunderstood. Abstaining from food with a spiritual goal and purpose will unleash the hidden power we all have as born-again Christians. But fasting and praying must be for a spiritual purpose, not for weight loss. *This book is my own small attempt to share my experiences as a prayer warrior for more than a decade.* The only caution I have is not to worry when things do not turn out the way you anticipated. Jesus reminded us that this is His Father's business, not even His. (He was speaking on a human level.) He told His earthly parents when He stayed behind in Jerusalem discussing the Law with the teachers of Law that He needed to stay behind because He was attending to His Father's business. It is God's business, and worrying is a false awareness that we know how God will respond or how things will turn out. We do not. The outcome is left with Him because the battle is the Lord's, and because the battle is His, He alone knows the results, and that part depends entirely on Him. So we pray that He fights for the results that will bring glory to His name. However, the only consolation, and it is a great consolation notwithstanding, is that a prayer warrior knows that God is in control and has the last word. Apostle Paul talks about the "surpassing greatness of His power for those who believe in Jesus Christ" (Ephesians 1:18–21). *So do not allow yourself to be threatened by any worries because the God you are serving as a prayer warrior is the one who reigns. His power is very prodigious, reassuring, and dependable. He is too faithful to fail you.*

The preceding discussion about the Holy Spirit's indispensable role in our prayer life should be explored by those who are eager to join this vocation for souls. The challenge is to know God personally or ask Him to reveal Himself to you. It is imperative to read the Word daily to acquaint yourself with Him and His will; to make praise a lifestyle; to ask daily for the gift and Spirit of faith; to witness to anyone, anywhere, under the right conditions; to remember that He is a sovereign God who knows everything there is to know because He creates reality; and finally to engage in secret prayer. To be victorious and triumphant over the powers of darkness, secret prayer must be part of your daily schedule.

I encourage you to use the God-given weapons to wit: the blood of Jesus, the fire of the Holy Ghost, the name of Jesus, the Word of God, the cross, and the most potent for a prayer warrior, praise. Praise always defeats the enemy.

Remember the following promises of the Bible. However, without a personal encounter or experience with Jesus Christ and His Spirit, we cannot expect these promises to prevail or outweigh the fears, that flow from the circumstances of life.

- "O Lord, God of our fathers, are you not the God who is in heaven? You rule over all the kingdoms of the nations, power and might are in your hand, and no one can withstand you; our God, did you not drive out the inhabitants of this land before your people Israel and gave it forever to the descendants of Abraham your friend?" (2 Chronicles 20:6–7).

- "And he believed in the Lord, and he counted it to him for righteousness" (Genesis 15:6).

- "And Abraham said unto God, O that Ishmael might live before thee" (Genesis 17:18).

- "And Abraham said my son, God will provide Himself a Lamb for a burnt offering: so, they went forth both of them together" (Genesis 22:8).

- "O Lord God of my master Abraham, I pray thee, send me good speed this day and shew kindness unto my master Abraham; Behold, I stand here by the well of water; and the daughters of the men of the city come out to draw water; And let it come to pass, that the damsel to whom I shall say; Let down thy pitcher, I pray thee, that I may drink and she shall say drink, and I will give thy camels drink also; let the same be she that thou has appointed for thy servant Isaac; and thereby shall I know that thou hast shewed kindness unto my master, And it came to pass, before he had done speaking, that behold, Rebekah came out, who was born to Bethuel, son of Milcah, the wife of Nahor, Abraham's brother, with her pitcher upon her shoulder" (Genesis 24:12–15).

- "Greater is He that is in you than he that is in the world" (1 John 4:4).

- "Cast thy burden unto the Lord; and He shall sustain thee" (Psalm 55:22).

- "My God shall supply all you need" (Philippians 4:19).

- "With men this is impossible, but with God all things are possible" (Matthew 19:26).

- "He that believeth on me, the works that I do he shall do also; and greater works than these shall he do; because I go to my father" (John 14:12).

- "The Holy Spirit abides in you, you know Him, for he dwells in you, and shall be in you" (John 14:16–17).

- "In my name ye shall cast out devils" (Mark 16:17).

- Ask for the Holy Spirit (Luke 11:13).

- "And they overcame him by the blood of the lamb and by the word of their testimony" (Revelation 12:11).

- "Fear not, neither be discouraged" (Deuteronomy 1:21).

- "What shall we then say to these things? If God be for us who can be against us?" (Romans 8:31).

- "Delight thyself also in the Lord; and He shall give thee the desires of thine heart" (Psalm 37:4).

- "None of them that trust in the Lord shall be desolate" (Psalm 34:22).

- "Submit to God, resist the devil and he shall flee from you" (James 4:7).

- "As thou hast believed, so be it done unto thee" (Matthew 8:13).

- "This is the day that the Lord has made: we will rejoice and be glad in it" (Psalm 118:24).

- "In all things and everything give thanks: for this is the will of God in Christ Jesus concerning you" (1 Thessalonians 5:18).

- "And the yoke shall be destroyed because of the anointing" (Isaiah 10:27).

- "But you have an unction from the Holy one" (1 John 2:20).

- "The anointing which you have received of Him abideth in you" (1 John 2:27).

- "Ask in the name of Jesus, it shall be done that the father may be glorified" (John 14:13–14).

- "Thou hast heard my voice, hide not thine ear at my cry" (Lamentations 3:56).

- "Ask in my name that your joy may be full" (John 16:24).

- "If you ask Him, He will cause you to hear His lovingkindness in the morning, and cause you to know the way wherein thou shall walk" (Psalm 143:8).

- Declare this when sick: Psalm 118:17.

- He blesses the righteous with favor (Psalm 5:12).

- Expect blessings from God, when you pray for your enemies (Job 42:10).

- "All my Springs are with thee" (Psalm 87:7).

- God is the Lord that has showed you light (Psalm 118:27).

- "Unto thee O Lord do I lift up my soul" (Psalm 25:1).

- "The eyes of the Lord are in every place" (Proverbs 15:3).

- "The Lord is a great God and a great King above all gods" (Psalm 95:3).

- "He performs the thing that is appointed for me" (Job 23:14).

- "In whose hand is the soul of every living thing" (Job 12:10).

- "Thy dominion is an everlasting dominion" (Daniel 4:34–35).

- "Power belongs to you, God" (Psalm 62:11).

- Nothing is impossible with Thee (Luke 1:37).

- "No one can thwart your plans for your people" (Job 42:2).

- "What thou has promised, thou art able also to perform" (Romans 4:21).

- "Hold up my goings in thy paths, that my footsteps slip not" (Psalm 17:5).

- "Be still and know that I am God" (Psalm 46:10).

- "Send out thy light and thy truth let them lead me" (Psalm 43:3).

- "I have set the Lord always before me; because He is at my right hand, I shall not be moved" (Psalm 16:8).

- "The Lord hear thee in the day of trouble" (Psalm 20:1).

- "Be thou exalted in thine own strength, so we will sing and praise thy power" (Psalm 21:13).

- "For thou art my rock and my fortress, therefore for thy great name's sake lead me and guide me" (Psalm 31:3).

- God is your portion forever, especially when your flesh and heart fail you (Psalm 73:26).

- Do you know who God says you are (Psalm 82:6)?

- His Lovingkindness and Mercy shall preserve you (Psalm 40:11).

- A peaceful life says a lot about you (Psalm 37:37).

- Do not go where He did not send you (Genesis 26:2–3).

- Is He your defense (Psalm 89:18)?

- Let the fire that surrounds Him be your portion (Psalm 97:3).

- Do you want to be restored (Psalm 80:3, 7, 19)?

- Are you weary? Go to Him; He has promised to give you rest (Matthew 11:28).

- Do you desire His beauty to be upon you (Psalm 90:17)?

- "Thou hast turned for me my mourning into dancing" (Psalm

30:11).

- "Thou art my hiding place; thou shall preserve me from trouble" (Psalm 32:7).

- "I will instruct thee and teach thee in the way which thou shall go, I will guide thee with mine eye" (Psalm 32:8).

- He is a gentleman (God is) and does not break His Covenant (Psalm 89:34).

- "Let thy mercy, O Lord be upon us, according as we hope in thee" (Psalm 33:22).

- He has given us everything that pertains to life and godliness (2 Peter 1:3).

- "Praise be to the Lord. The God of Israel from everlasting to everlasting" (Psalm 106:48).

- "The Lord reigns forever" (Psalm 146:10).

- Give thanks to Him and praise His name (Psalm 100:4).

- Praise the Lord because He has done great things for us (Psalm 126:2–3).

- "Surely the Lord is in this place, and I never knew it" (Genesis 28:16).

- He invites you to rejoice in His name (Psalm 89:16).

- Do you have adversaries (Psalm 71:13)?

- He has given commandment to save you (Psalm 71:3).

- Man's help is vaporous (Psalm 60:11).

- Ask God to speak to your children when you notice any incipient form of rebellion (Psalm 29:4).

- He delivers the poor and needy when they cry to Him (Psalm 72:12).

- He wants you to trust Him at all times (Psalm 62:8).

- Ask God to send His fear to go before you and cause your enemies to turn their backs and flee from you (Exodus 23:27).

- He has multiple ways to defeat your enemies on your behalf (Genesis 35:5).

- He is the one that makes you perfect while you do His will (Hebrews 13:20–21).

- Always give God the credit for using the gifts He gave you (Genesis 41:16).

- Do not hesitate to give Him glory or He will curse your blessings (Malachi 2:2).

- His love toward you is better than life itself (Psalm 63:3).

- God is the one who brings down your enemies (Psalm 60:12).

- Bless Him, and He will do wonders in your life (Psalm 72:18).

- He will never turn away your prayers (Psalm 66:20).

- Until He delivers you, you cannot walk before Him (Psalm 56:13).

- Did you know that He has blessed you to approach Him (Psalm 65:4)?

- Has He been of help to you (Psalm 63:7)?

- Did you know that He has pledged to comfort you on every side (Psalm 71:21)?

- Praise is the secret. You cannot perform what He expects from you until you develop a lifestyle of praise (Psalm 61:8).

- The secret of the Lord is with them that revere Him, and to them will He show his plan (Psalm 25:14).

- "Man shall not live by bread alone, but by every word that proceeds from the mouth of God" (Matthew 4:4).

- God uses simple things to confound your enemies (2 Kings 7:6).

- It is the Lord that gives conception (Ruth 4:13).

- The eternal God is our refuge (Deuteronomy 33:27).

- God can command the stars to fight against your enemies (Judges 5:20).

- "Heaven and earth shall pass away, but my words shall not pass away" (Matthew 24:35).

- Have I been a wilderness to you (Jeremiah 2:31)?

- God will go before you every day (Deuteronomy 31:8).

- Do not fear your enemies because He will fight for you (Deuteronomy 3:22).

- Accept invitations to go with God's people because you will receive the same blessings that they will get (Numbers 10:32).

- When God sends you, go because He will speak for you (Exodus 4:12).

- God will make you prosper as long as you seek Him (2 Chronicles 26:5).

- Call on God, and He will bless you (Jabez did) (1 Chronicles 4:10).

- God will make room for you if you are patient and peaceful and give your own Rehoboth (Genesis 26:22).

- Do not fear anything, because the thing you are afraid of may actually happen (Job 3:25).

- "I will say of the Lord, He is my refuge and my fortress in Him shall I trust" (Psalm 91:2).

- "Say ye to the righteous, it shall be well with you" (Isaiah 3:10).

- "For His eyes are open upon the ways of man, and He sees all his goings" (Job 34:21).

- "And it shall come to pass, that before they call, I will answer" (Isaiah 65:24).

- "Keep thy heart with all diligence, for out of it are the issues of life" (Proverbs 4:23).

- "The Lord shall fight for you and ye shall hold your peace" (Exodus 14:14).

- Deal with your fellowman as a brother and a sister because you all have one father (Malachi 2:10).

- "Nevertheless, He saved them for His name's sake, that He might make His mighty power to be known" (Psalm 106:8).

- Life is a gift from God (Romans 6:23).

- "Known unto God are all his works, from the beginning of the world" (Acts 15:18).

- "Great peace have they which love thy Law, nothing shall offend them" (Psalm 119:165).

- "As I live, saith the Lord, I have no pleasure in the death of the wicked" (Ezekiel 33:11).

- "Because thou hast rejected the word of the Lord, He hast also rejected thee from being King" (1 Samuel 15:23).

- "Since I was with you, lacked ye anything [Luke 22:35]?"

- "The name of the Lord is a strong tower; the righteous runs into it and are safe" (Proverbs 18:10).

- "They that trust in the Lord shall be as mount Zion, which cannot be removed, but abideth forever" (Psalm 125:1).

- "As the mountains are round about Jerusalem, so the Lord is round about his people from henceforth even forever" (Psalm 125:2).

- "The Lord is my Shepherd, I shall not want" (Psalm 23:1).

- "I am the Lord, your redeemer and creator. I made all things, the earth and all things in it [Isaiah 44:24]."

- "I am the God who confirms the words of my servants [Isaiah 44:26]."

- Who has delivered you from the power of darkness and has translated you into the kingdom of His dear Son (Colossians 1:13)?

- "Who forgiveth all thine iniquities and heals all thy diseases" (Psalm 103:3).

- Lay claim only to what is given to you from heaven (John 3:37).

- "Oh, satisfy us early with thy mercy; that we may rejoice and be glad all our days" (Psalm 90:14).

- "If my people will pray, I will forgive their sins [2 Chronicles 7:14]."

- "Ask counsel, we pray thee of God that we may know we are on the path of prosperity" (Judges 18:5).

- "With thanksgiving let your requests be made known unto God" (Philippians 4:6).

- "My voice shall thou hear in the morning, O Lord" (Psalm 5:3).

- Pray and make supplications (2 Chronicles 6:24).

- "Finally, my brethren, be strong in the Lord. And in the power of His might" (Ephesians 6:10–12).

- When you talk about other members of your congregation behind their backs (the spirit of gossip; busybodies), you become a character without use to God (2 Corinthians 12:20).

- "Whatsoever ye ask in prayer, believe, ye shall receive" (Matthew 21:22).

- "To all which believe, He is precious" (1 Peter 2:7).

- "Behold, God is my salvation; I will trust, and not be afraid" (Isaiah 12:2).

- "Ye have not because ye ask not" (James 4:2).

- "Hast thou faith? Have it to thyself before God" (Romans 14:22).

- "He is faithful that promised" (Hebrews 10:23).

- "He has inclined His ear unto me, therefore will I call upon Him" (Psalm 116:2).

- "For the blood of Jesus cleanses us from all sins" (1 John 1:7).

- Sing unto the Lord with thanksgiving (Psalm 147:7).

- "I love the Lord because He has heard my voice" (Psalm 116:1).

- "This is the love of God, that we keep His commandments" (1 John 5:3)

- "Continue in prayer and watch" (Colossians 4:2).

- "The Lord hath dealt bountifully with thee" (Psalm 116:7).

- Let them that love Thy name be joyful in Thee (Psalm 5:11).

- "Make the voice of His praise to be heard" (Psalm 66:8).

- He will be our guide even unto death (Psalm 48:14).

- "God forbid that I should sin in ceasing to pray for you" (1 Samuel 12:23).

- "Seek ye first the Kingdom of God and His righteousness, and all these things shall be added unto you" (Matthew 6:33).

- Ask God, and He will give it to thee (John 11:22).

- "Trust him with all thine heart and lean not unto thy own understanding and He shall direct thy paths" (Proverbs 3:5–6).

- "The Lord is good to the soul that seeketh Him" (Lamentations 3:25).

- "We are more than conquerors through Him who loved us" (Romans 8:37).

- "He knoweth our frame; He remembereth that we are dust" (Psalm 103:14).

- "We are bound to thank God always" (2 Thessalonians 1:8).

- "God resisteth the proud, but giveth grace unto the humble" (James 4:6).

- "I will extol thee my God, O King: and I will bless thy Name for ever and ever; every day will I bless thee, and I will praise thy name for ever and ever" (Psalm 145:1–4).

- "Hear O Lord, when I cry with my voice" (Psalm 27:7).

- "The Lord preserveth the faithful" (Psalm 31:23).

- "The Lord is the strength of my life" (Psalm 27:1).

- "They shall prosper that love thee" (Psalm 122:6).

- "I will give thee thanks forever" (Psalm 30:12).

- "The prayer of faith shall save" (James 5:15).

- "Thanks be to God for His unspeakable gift" (2 Corinthians 9:15).

- "I was brought low, He helped me" (Psalm 116:6).

- "Let those that seek thee rejoice and be glad in thee" (Psalm 70:4).

- "Thy prayers and thine alms are come up before God" (Acts 10:4).

- "Whoso offereth praise glorifieth Me" (Psalm 50:23).

- "Save me for thy mercies' sake" (Psalm 31:16).

- "We trust in the Living God, the Savior of all men" (1 Timothy 4:10).

- "We love Him because He first loved us" (1 John 4:19).

- "I have loved thee with an everlasting love" (Jeremiah 31:3).

- "For thy Name's sake, lead me and guide me" (Psalm 31:3).

- "The Lord shall guide thee continually" (Isaiah 58:11).

- "Blessed is the man that maketh the Lord his trust" (Psalm 40:4).

- "I will magnify Him with thanksgiving" (Psalm 69:30).

- "O thou that hearest prayer, unto thee shall all flesh come" (Psalm 65:2).

- "If a man love me, he will keep my words" (John 14:23).

- He shall save them because they trust in Him (Psalm 37:40).

- "Remember the Sabbath day (Saturday) to keep it holy" (Exodus 20:8–9).

- "I am the living bread which came down from heaven; if any man eat of this bread, he shall live forever" (John 6:51).

- "I am the bread of Life, he that cometh to me shall never hunger; and he that believeth on me shall never thirst" (John 6:35).

- "This is His commandment, that we believe on the name of his Son Jesus Christ and Love one another" (1 John 3:23).

- "Thou Lord art good and ready to forgive" (Psalm 86:5).

- "Unite my heart to fear thy name" (Psalm 86:11).

- "Mine eyes shall be upon the faithful of the land" (Psalm 101:6).

- "The just shall live by his faith" (Habakkuk 2:4).

- "He will love thee and bless thee" (Deuteronomy 7:13).

- "Let the people praise thee O God; Let all the people praise thee" (Psalm 67:5–7).

- "Casting all your care upon Him; for He careth for you" (1 Peter 5:7).

- "Rest in the Lord, and wait patiently for Him" (Psalm 37:7).

- "Thou art my God and I will praise thee" (Psalm 118:28).

- "Knock and it shall be opened on to you" (Luke 11:9).

- "We thank thee, and praise thy glorious name" (1 Chronicles 29:13).

- "If thou seek Him, He will be found of thee" (1 Chronicles 28:9).

- "The hand of our God is upon all them for good that seek Him" (Ezra 8:22).

- If ye forgive, your Father will forgive you (Matthew 6:14).

- "Thou Lord hast not forsaken them that seek thee" (Psalm 9:10).

- "If thou canst believe, all things are possible" (Mark 9:23).

- "Unto thee, O Lord do I lift up my soul" (Psalm 86:2).

- "The love of God is shed abroad in our hearts" (Romans 5:5).

- "Without faith, it is impossible to please God" (Hebrew 11:6).

- "He that trusteth in the Lord, mercy shall compass him about" (Psalm 32:10).

- "Let the poor and the needy praise thy name" (Psalm 74:21).

- "The Lord knoweth them that trust Him" (Nahum 1:7).

- "The God of love and peace shall be with you" (2 Corinthians 13:11).

- "My tongue shall speak of thy righteousness and praise" (Psalm 35:28).

- "Ye are my friends, if ye do whatsoever I command you" (John 15:14).

- "Let us lay aside…the sin, which doth so easily beset us" (Hebrew 12:1).

- "Lord increase our faith" (Luke 17:5).

- He has pledged to beat down your foes before your face (Psalm

89:23).

- "Create in me a clean heart…and renew a right Spirit within me" (Psalm 51:10).

- "Except the Lord build the house, they labor in vain that built it" (Psalm 27:1).

- "My grace is sufficient for thee" (2 Corinthians 12:9).

- Purpose to sing of His mercy and power because He has been your defense and refuge in the day of your trouble (Psalm 59:16).

- Call upon Him in the day of trouble, and He shall deliver you; but don't forget to glorify Him (Psalm 50:15).

- He has made you stronger than all your enemies (Psalm 105:24).

- He is plenteous in mercy and slow to anger (Psalm 103:8).

- "Neglect not the gift that is in thee" (1 Timothy 4:14).

- "Therefore, if any man be in Christ, he is a new creature" (2 Corinthians 5:17).

- "Ye shall know the truth, and the truth shall make you free" (John 8:32).

- To them that received and believed Him, He gave the power to become the Sons of God (John 1:12).

- "Lo, I am with you always even unto the end of the world" (Matthew 28:20).

- "I have set before you life and death" (Deuteronomy 30:19).

- "I am come that they might have life" (John 10:10).

- "This poor man cried, and the Lord heard him, and saved him out of all his troubles" (Psalm 34:6).

- "The Lord shall be thy confidence" (Proverbs 3:26).

- "And He said, My presence shall go with thee and give thee rest"

(Exodus 33:14).

- "Lead us not into temptation but deliver us from evil" (Matthew 6:13).

- "I will bless the Lord at all times" (Psalm 34:1).

- "He forgeteth not the cry of the humble" (Psalm 9:12).

- "Believe in the Lord your God" (2 Chronicles 20:20).

- "He heareth the prayer of the righteous" (Proverbs 15:29).

- Wait on the Lord, and He shall renew thy strength (Isaiah 40:31).

- He is able to keep you from falling (Jude 1:24).

- "Let God be magnified" (Psalm 70:4).

- He sends His angel to go before you and bring you in the place He has prepared (Exodus 23:20).

- We must learn to pray like King David of old: "Lord turn the counsel of my enemies into foolishness" (2 Samuel 15:31).

- The Lord is always mindful of His people to bless them (Psalm 115:12).

- "Evening, and morning, and at noon, will I pray" (Psalm 55:17).

- "Have faith in God" (Mark 11:22).

- What Jesus tells you is for your guidance (John 14:25–26).

- What Jesus taught is our message to others (Matthew 28:19–20).

- Let no man take thy crown through carelessness, gossip in the church, or fighting for positions in the church, because crowns are lost and won in the common ways of life. This crown is a crown of righteousness (2 Timothy 4:8).

- He is just and "renderest to every man according to his work" (Psalm 62:12).

- "It is better to trust in the Lord than to put confidence in man" (Psalm 118:8).

- "This is the victory that overcometh the world, even our faith" (1 John 5:4).

- "The Lord is a sun and shield" (Psalm 84:11).

- Do not be dishonest with God and your fellow man (Acts 5:1–10).

- "I called upon the Lord in distress: the Lord answered me" (Psalm 118:5).

- "Do not let sin reign in your mortal body" (Romans 6:12).

- "He is a buckler to all them that trust in Him" (2 Samuel 22:31).

- "O thou my God, save thy servant that trusteth in thee" (Psalm 86:2).

- "Whoso putteth his trust in the Lord shall be safe" (Proverbs 29:25).

- "Come into His presence with thanksgiving" (Psalm 95:2).

- "Let no corrupt communication come out of your mouth" (Ephesians 4:29–31).

- "Happy is he that hath the God of Jacob for his help" (Psalm 146:5).

- "He is faithful and just to forgive us our sins" (1 John 1:9).

- "Thou art my God; early will I seek thee" (Psalm 63:1).

- Put the claims of Jesus into practice, and you will become impregnable (Matthew 7:24–25).

- "If thou faint in the day of adversity, thy strength is small" (Proverbs 24:10).

- "Her sins, which are many, are forgiven" (Luke 7:47).

- "If we ask anything according to His will, He heareth us" (1 John 5:14).

- "The prayer of the upright is His delight" (Proverbs 15:8).

- "Commit thy way unto the Lord" (Psalm 37:5).

- What Jesus said is fundamental to fellowship with God (John 14:23–24).

- "The Lord shall preserve thy going out and thy coming in" (Psalm 121:8).

- "Let thine hand help me for I have chosen thy precepts" (Psalm 119:173).

- "The Lord is thy keeper" (Psalm 121:5).

- The Lord is the Lord of heaven and earth (Acts 17:24).

- "There is none like me in all the earth" (Exodus 9:14).

- "For they shall eat and not have enough, they shall commit harlotry but not increase, because they have ceased obeying the Lord" (Hosea 4:10).

- Give Him your heart, and He will give you power to observe His ways (Proverbs 23:26).

- Let the Lord reward those who do evil to you (2 Timothy 4:14).

- The Lord has pledged to deliver you from every evil work (2 Timothy 4:18).

- No strength can deliver a mighty man, and no king can be saved by a multitude of an army (Psalm 33:16).

- Remember, a man's life is not defined by the things he owns (Luke 12:15).

- "There is no lack to them that fear and seek Him" (Psalm 34:9–10).

- Do not be misled by the glamour, glitter, and attractions of this present world (2 Timothy 4:10).

- "Beside me, there is no other God. I am the first and last [Isaiah

44:6]."

- Blessed is the man that trusts and has confidence in Jehovah (Jeremiah 17:7).

- "Thou hast been a shelter for me and a strong tower from my enemy" (Psalm 61:3).

- "The blessings of the Lord, it maketh rich, and addeth no sorrow to it" (Proverbs 10:22).

- "Seven times a day do I praise thee because of thy righteous judgments" (Psalm 119:164).

- "At midnight I will rise to give thanks because of thy righteous judgments" (Psalm 119:62).

- "Be not afraid, only believe" (Mark 5:36).

- Search me, try me, and see if there be any wickedness in me, and lead me in the way everlasting (Psalm 139:23–24).

- "For I know that the Lord is great and above all gods" (Psalm 135:5).

- In a crisis—and indeed, in any crisis—remember that your status as a child of the king does *not* change (Daniel 6:10).

- "The Lord shall preserve thee from all evil" (Psalm 121:7).

- "Let mine adversaries be clothed with shame and let them cover themselves with their own confusion" (Psalm 109:29).

- He loadeth us with benefits daily (Psalm 68:19).

- "O earth, earth, earth, hear the word of the Lord" (Jeremiah 22:29).

- "And I will deliver thee out of the hand of the wicked" (Jeremiah 15:21).

- "And they shall fight against thee, but they shall not prevail against thee, for I am with thee" (Jeremiah 1:19).

- Because God is with you, your persecutors shall stumble and not prevail (Jeremiah 20:11).

- It is not by your might or strength, but by God's Spirit that you prevail (Zechariah 4:6).

- He is always with you and comes with His love (Zephaniah 3:17).

- "My kindness I shall not take from you [Isaiah 54:10]."

- "I will go before thee and make crooked places straight" (Isaiah 45:2).

- He shall send a blast upon your enemies, and they shall fall by their own sword (Isaiah 37:7).

- "Thou wilt keep him in perfect peace, whose mind is stayed on thee; because he trusts in thee" (Isaiah 26:3).

- God is a strength to the poor and to the needy (Isaiah 25:4).

- He ordains peace for his people (Isaiah 26:12).

- Man is made after the similitude of God (James 3:9).

- "He hath said, I will never leave the: nor forsake thee; so that we may boldly say, The Lord is my helper, I will not fear what man can do unto me" (Hebrews 13:5–6).

- "The Lord is the true God; He is the Living God and an everlasting King" (Jeremiah 10:10).

- "Though he slay me, yet will I trust in Him" (Job 13:15).

- Take counsel against God's people, and it shall come to nought (Isaiah 8:10).

- He will give you His Spirit if you obey Him (Acts 5:32).

- We ought to obey God rather than man (Acts 5:29).

- You cannot overthrow God's agenda; you will be fighting with God and can never win (Acts 5:38–39).

- A heathen king saw the power of the living God and could not help but testify about Him (Daniel 3:29).

- If you are a preacher, please preach and teach Jesus (Acts 5:42).

- "Woe to the wicked, for the reward of his hands shall be given him" (Isaiah 3:11).

- "Plead the cause of the poor and needy" (Proverbs 31:9).

- "Let my mouth be filled with thy praise" (Psalm 71:8).

- "Ye are servants of righteousness" (Romans 6:18).

- "God said, Ask what I shall give thee" (1 Kings 3:5).

- "Forgive and ye shall be forgiven" (Luke 6:37).

- "He disappoints the devices of the crafty so that their hands cannot perform their enterprise" (Job 5:12).

- "He that giveth to the poor shall not lack" (Proverbs 28:27).

- God performs all things for you (Psalm 57:1–2).

- You and I cannot do anything for God, unless He gives you a new heart and a new spirit (Ezekiel 36:26–28).

- "The law of the Lord is perfect, converting the soul" (Psalm 19:7).

- "Preserve me O God, for in thee do I put my trust" (Psalm 16:1).

- Loyalty to God does not go uncompensated (Matthew 19:29).

- Do not conform; the three young Hebrew boys, in their refusal to conform, stuck out and stood out like the proverbial sore thumb, and you can too (Daniel 3:16–18).

- "I have made the earth and created man upon it" (Isaiah 45:12).

- "Give ear, O ye heavens, and I will speak and hear O earth the word of my mouth" (Deuteronomy 32:1).

- "In the way of righteousness is life and, in the pathway, thereof, there is no death" (Proverbs 12:28).

- Committing adultery destroys your own soul, and a wound and dishonor you shall get. And your reproach shall never be wiped away (Proverbs 6:32–33).

- "His ears are open unto our prayers" (1 Peter 3:12).

- "Thou hast granted me life and favor and thy visitation hath preserved my spirit" (Job 10:12).

- "The Spirit of God hath made me and the breath of the Almighty hath given me life" (Job 33:4).

- "Thou shall also decree a thing and it shall be established unto thee" (Job 22:28).

- We have peace with God through our Lord Jesus Christ (Romans 5:1).

- "Giving thanks always for all things unto God and the Father in the name of our Lord Jesus Christ" (Ephesians 5:20).

- "The Lord is good to all; and his tender mercies are over all His works" (Psalm 145:9).

- God gives those who are *good in His sight wisdom, knowledge,* and *joy* (Ecclesiastes 2:26).

As prayer warriors, we are called to a work that human power cannot accomplish; Only the abiding presence of the Holy Spirit can produce a life that will empower us to influence the world as the "salt of the earth."

That is why it is profitable to summarize that in all of this, we have a starting point, and that is *"You are not alone." The Holy Spirit is with you. It is reassuring and a life-changing certainty.* If you do not believe me, listen to this: "Let your conversation be without covetousness, and be content with such things as ye have, for He has said, I will *never* leave thee, nor forsake thee. So that we may boldly *say* the Lord is my helper and I will not fear what man shall do unto me" (Hebrews 13:5–6). In the book of 1 John 4:15, Scripture says, "Anyone who confesses that Jesus is the Son of God, God dwells in Him, and he dwells in God." And if God dwells in you, who can be against you? Nothing and nobody. God is just a confession away.

Returning to the central theme as stated at the beginning: the Holy Spirit is who we need to serve God as prayer warriors. When Jesus was asked what it would take to do the works of God? He said in John 6:28–29 that having faith on the one whom God has sent, and that was Himself. But because of the misunderstanding that exists among some Christians, it is completely safe to say that God's work is what we allow God to do through us and not what we do for God. He is indispensable in everything we do for Christ. That is the greatest need of the church of the twenty-first century. When Jesus said the gates of hell could never prevail against His church, what I think He had in mind was that the church that the Holy Spirit possesses is the church that would be impregnable in these last days. How do you do that? By making sure that He is invited in every endeavor that the church is involved in whether in children's stories, Sunday school or Sabbath school discussions, prayer meetings, hospital and prison visits, sermons, evangelistic crusades, or choir practices. We must invite Him to take control. The only condition for receiving the Holy Spirit is to ask for Him. "If you, then, being evil know how to give good gifts to your children, how much more will *your* heavenly Father give the Holy Spirit to those who ask Him!" (Luke 11:13). Asking is the condition for receiving Him.

Now all this depends on whether you believe in the good report. The good report is the Word of God. Let us ask for the Spirit of obedience to apply the Word of God daily in our lives because it is our daily interaction and response to the Word of God and the Holy Spirit that capacitates our faith in God. I experienced the power in the Word of God several years back when I got my first job as a family nurse practitioner in Birmingham, Alabama. I lived in Huntsville and drove every day to Birmingham, ninety-nine miles. I learned that when the Bible speaks, God speaks. About fifty miles into Birmingham one morning on my way to work, my car broke down. I sat in my car and prayed from Psalm 20:1–2, where the Bible says, "The Lord hear thee in the day of trouble; the name of the God of Jacob defend thee; send thee help from the sanctuary and strengthen thee out of Zion." At the end of that prayer, I said, "Lord do as thou has said in your word because I need help right now." What happened next was a miracle that I would never forget as long as I live. No sooner did I say amen, than a guy in a red truck stopped behind me and asked if I needed help. The guy was a mechanic who knew how to repair cars. He opened the hood of my car and immediately told me what was wrong and helped me to buy a new battery from a nearby Walmart. He told me that my alternator was the problem. The time between my amen and when the young Samaritan (mechanic) appeared to inquire whether I needed help was the miracle. As soon as I said amen, he appeared. In response to my prayer, God did not just send someone to help me but sent a mechanic. Prayer warriors should read the word and memorize the promises of God and apply them to circumstances that they face in their daily lives. Give back God's word to Him in your prayers, and implore Him to fulfill His word in your life because He watches His Word to perform it (Jeremiah 1:12). *His supply to our needs at any given time is always seasonable and unfailing. In fact, it works especially when you put your trust in His Word.*

In Numbers 13, two spies came back with a good report because of their faith. Ten came back with a not-so-good report. The irony is that they saw the same challenges. What made the difference between the two spies with the good report and those with the not-so-good report? Here is my ratiocination. The beauty of prayer warriors' lives exudes from their knowledge of God that depends on their daily contact with His Word and the Holy Spirit. Those with the excellent report had daily contact with the Holy Spirit and His Word, and the ten spies with the negative report were perfunctory Christians. The two spies were aware of the promise, which says nothing shall be impossible with God. They knew that the battle was always the Lord's. But more importantly, the church of the twenty-first century should not ignore the Holy Spirit's role in reaching the lost. It is that perspective and mindset that should characterize prayer warriors and the church of the twenty-first century. I hope that these chapters will increase and deepen your interaction with the Holy Spirit as you allow Him to open your understanding as you read and study the word, fast, and pray for souls.

My goal has been to impress upon my readers that the Holy Spirit is indispensable in everything that the church of the twenty-first century does. If we must seriously think of participating in the gospel commission, then we must also know and understand that nothing can be accomplished for Christ without the Holy Spirit's influence and power. In the book of Zechariah 4:6, God Himself says it is not by might nor by power, but by my Spirit. Every prayer warrior and all the churches of the twenty-first century interested in witnessing for Christ before His Second Coming must believe in the power of the Holy Spirit. It is worthless to rely on human resources, human strength, and human intuition or sagacity. Relying on the Holy Spirit guarantees His presence and power, and therefore victory and success.

I think that I have sought to make a scrupulously accurate case of the important role that the Holy Spirit must play in witnessing for Christ. I hope that this contributes to our increased ability to reach more souls for Christ to the glory of God. That is the underlying objective of this writing, and I believe God will be pleased, and our value to Him would be enhanced. And by this, I mean our usefulness.

Occasionally, lions do roar, and even the deaf can hear.
Abide with me:
Abide with me, fast falls the eventide;
The darkness deepens, Lord, with me abide
When other helpers fail and comforts flee
Help of the helpless, oh, abide with me
The last words…
"Let us hear the conclusion of the whole matter: Fear God and keep His commandments: for this is the whole duty of man" (Ecclesiastes 12:13).

These instructions and discussion represent a desire to revive the supernatural today that characterized the ethos of the first century church with such moving and memorable results. Christianity is a supernatural religion, and the natural becomes supernatural when we allow God, the Holy Spirit, to get involved in His business. What prayer warriors represent is a willingness to participate in interceding for lost souls. In the book of Isaiah 59:16 (Good News Bible), God saw and wondered that there were no intercessors to help the oppressed. So He decided to use His own power to rescue them and win the victory.

Here is the irony. He has given us that power through His Spirit as a gift. And that gift is without measure. In other words, abundantly (John 3:34). Furthermore, the Holy Spirit is a permanent gift (John 14:16; 2 John 2).

What we have talked about so far in the book are instructions on how to do it the right way. Now let us talk about the gospel or the good news. This good news is not considered good until you start sharing it. You must believe what Jesus said when He stated in Matthew 21:22, "And all things whatsoever ye shall ask in prayer, believing ye shall receive." This is from the one who upholds the world with His word (Hebrews 1:3) and who speaks, and it is done. When He commands, it stands still (Psalm 33:9). Faith in God, His word, and the power of the Holy Spirit, are the greatest realities to a prayer warrior. John the apostle writes to the churches in Asia Minor (1 John 5:4–5), and I would let him speak for himself as he states, "For whatsoever is born of God overcomes the world, and this is the victory that overcomes the world: even our faith and who is he that overcomes the world, but he that believeth that Jesus is the Son of God." However, we may not be judged by what we believe because even the devils believe but by what changes our belief has wrought in our lives. That is why the greatest blessing a prayer warrior experiences as he or she seeks the lost for Christ is that their own character through the transforming power of God's grace makes them fit for eternity. They pray and ask God to change their lives to fit the message and meet His standards and demands that they are sharing. That is an important consideration for those eager to join this band of intercessors. Prayer warriors are always praying for souls. Everyone in this life/world is considered a soul. Prostitutes, pastors, presidents, evangelists, children, those on drugs, atheists, homosexuals, backsliders, those contemplating suicide, young adults leaving or thinking of leaving the church, and unconverted Christians in the church to name but a few. And when you pray for other people, God shapes your character and gives you His mind. "Let this mind be in you as it was in Christ Jesus" (Philippians 2:5).

You must believe that Jesus is the Son of God. In the same epistle in chapter 4:15, and we talked about this earlier, John the apostle says, "Whosoever shall confess that Jesus is the Son of God, God dwells in him and he in God." This means that when we go out to seek freedom for the oppressed or to participate in the great commission to set the captives free or pray for them on our knees in our homes, we have all heaven with us. That is very comforting and reassuring that we cannot lose.

Second, remember the blood of Jesus is what overcomes the devil. Plead the blood of Jesus as you meet with these oppressed souls. And because they are under the power of the devil, he will not let them go without a fight. Scripture says we overcome the evil one with the blood of the lamb (Revelation 12:11). The blood of Jesus avers eternally to the devil's defeat (Colossians 2:14–15; Hebrews 2:14). It is very important to know that every challenge you encounter is a sign that you are becoming a danger to the devil. Be encouraged because he is a defeated foe.

Have faith in the name of Jesus and take the name of Jesus with you. It is a name that is above every other name, and I have come to the settled conclusion that the name of Jesus always disrupts the plans of the devil (Acts 3:6,16). Be confident that the Holy Spirit (counselor for the defense) is your invisible ally. As you iterate and develop your strategy to participate in the great commission, as you enlist the power of the Holy Spirit, your role is to do the praying and let Him be your God. That I have found to be the best strategy.

This last point or strategy may not be very popular. It is found in Isaiah 30:31, and it says, "For through the voice of the Lord shall the Assyrians be beaten down, which smote with a rod." Ask the Lord to speak to the souls you intend to visit. Ask Him to give you access to their hearts and minds. Psalms 29 says the voice of the Lord is powerful and majestic. Let God speak to these people before you talk to them. Remember, with God all things are possible, and you can do all things through Christ who strengthens you. In the end, prayer is the defining activity of a true church. A praying church is a place where there is unity among the members. And the secret of unity in the church is where the equality of the believers is fostered because that is where God pours out His blessings (Psalm 133:1–3).

Power in the blood
Would you be free from the burden of sin?
There's power in the blood, power in the blood.

Would you O'er evil a victory win?
There's wonderful power in the blood
Refrain
There is power, power, wonder-working power
In the blood of the Lamb.
There's power, power, wonder-working power
In the precious blood of the Lamb.

As you go
The Lord bless thee, and keep thee
The Lord make His face, shine upon thee, and be
    gracious unto thee
The Lord lift up His countenance upon thee, and
    give thee peace
And they shall put my name upon the children of
    Israel, and I will bless them.
Numbers 6:24–27

ENDORSEMENT

This book, *Facts and Interpretations*, Charles has written from the premise that facts in the Bible can be interpreted correctly only as we develop and cultivate a genuine relationship with God through the Holy Spirit by communing with God through prayer. Perhaps the greatest strength of this book is Charles's unrelenting emphasis that prayer is about God, talking to God, praying and doing God's will, and God being a priority in prayer.

Charles delves into the subject of prayer, which is so pertinent to our spirituality and being effective witnesses of God but often not given much attention or casually carried out or misunderstood. Weaving through the Word of God and personal experience as a prayer warrior, Charles writes as a "witness" to the importance and power of prayer. In his writing, he also attempts to create a composite portrait of who is a prayer warrior.

In this book, Charles encapsulates the key to a prayer warrior's effectiveness in prayer—"a consecrated prayer life of the prayer warrior and reminds us that prayer flows out of an intimate relationship with our heavenly Father." As you read this book, you will both be encouraged and challenged to examine your prayer life and personal relationship with God.

Right after Paul prayed for the Ephesians to "have strength to comprehend with all the saints what is the breadth and length and height and depth…the love of Christ that surpasses knowledge" (Eph. 3:18–19), he reminded the church that God had given them pastors and teachers to equip them for every good work (Eph. 4:11–12). In this book, Charles is a teacher equipping you for every good work, soli Deo gloria (for glory to God alone).

Any prayer warrior who wants to learn more about prayer or improve their prayer life or enhance their understanding of prayer will find this book an important resource to equip him/her on that firm foundation, to commit yourself to prayer with confidence that God is willing and able to hear and answer your prayers.

This is a short, simple, practical book not just for prayer warriors but for everyone seeking intimacy with God through prayer.

Dr. Fenades Obinchu
Senior Pastor, Dallas International and
Dallas Newlife SDA churches, Texas

ABOUT THE AUTHOR

Misori, Charles, earned a BA degree in philosophy and religion, BSN, MSN (clinical nurse specialist) post-MSN (family nurse practitioner), and a PhD in community health.

He has served as a prayer coordinator for well over thirteen years in his local SDA church in Alabama. Furthermore, he has also provided spiritual services as the chaplain for the North Alabama Prayer Foundation for well over ten years. In addition, he is an ordained Elder in the Seventh-day Adventist church.

It is while serving in these capacities that he learned that the Holy Spirit is indispensable in prayer and that Jesus spoke about prayer to those who "believe." And those who believe do not allow their thoughts about God to be too human.

www.ingramcontent.com/pod-product-compliance
Lightning Source LLC
Chambersburg PA
CBHW051234120626
46547CB00013B/1640

* 9 7 9 8 8 9 3 5 6 2 1 2 5 *